ADD KIDS, STIR BRISKLY
OR
HOW I LEARNED TO LOVE MY LIFE

Jo and Hiroshi. (COURTESY OF VALERIE STETSON)

Dear Janet,

We hope this will give you a few laughs, while you're "mending."

Love, Lynne, Rob, Robby + Jaimee

ADD KIDS, STIR BRISKLY

OR
HOW I LEARNED TO LOVE MY LIFE

Jo Owens

Jo Owens

Horsdal & Schubart

Horsdal & Schubart Publishers Ltd.
Victoria, BC, Canada

Cover: Original painting by John Climenhage, Victoria, BC, and Peterborough, Ontario. Image manipulation by Dirk Keller, Island Graphics, Victoria, BC.

This book is set in Aldine 401 Book Text.

We acknowledge the support of the Canada Council for the Arts for our publishing program.
We also acknowledge the assistance of the Province of British Columbia, through the British Columbia Arts Council.

Printed and bound in Canada by Printcrafters, Winnipeg, Manitoba.

Canadian Cataloguing in Publication Data

Owens, Jo, 1961-
 Add kids, stir briskly, or, How I learned to love my life

ISBN 0-920663-66-4

 1. Owens, Jo, 1961- . 2. Mothers—Biography. 3. Mother and child.
I. Title. II. Title: How I learned to love my life.
HQ759.O93 1999   306.874'3'092   C99-910275-3

Printed and bound in Canada

Dedicated (as I am) to M'hoo and the two
with love

Mama Jo

ACKNOWLEDGMENTS

With heartfelt thanks to:
* Mom, for absolutely everything.
* Grace, for being my inspiration and my muse.
* H.G., for being there when it all started. Good luck and bless you.
* Susan, for reading the weekly installment and encouraging me every step of the way. Couldn't have got up so early without you!
* Shirley-the-Amazing, for endless support, use of the printer and showing me the next step in the parenting process.
* All the readers who suffered through the first draft and cheered me on, especially Leslie, out of the blue.
* Justine, for picking up the phone.
* Kathy, for the title.
* The staff at the P.I.C.U., with my eternal gratitude.
* Mas and Kay for all their help (especially the computer!).
* All my friends and community for sustenance.
* Marlyn and Michael, for taking a chance.
* And last, but not least, to all my aunts, especially Margaret, who once told me, "You're flakier than breakfast cereal, but it will make you a good writer someday." Wish you were here.

The history of every major Galactic Civilization tends to pass through three distinct and recognizable phases, those of Survival, Inquiry and Sophistication, otherwise known as the How, Why and Where phases.

For instance, the first phase is characterized by the question *How can we eat?* the second by the question *Why do we eat?* and the third by the question *Where shall we have lunch?*

from *The Hitch Hiker's Guide to the Galaxy*
by Douglas Adams

RECIPES

ONE

This is bad: when PMS coincides with the monthly bills coming in. Emotional vulnerability on a date with financial reality.

I never planned to have kids. In fact, I planned not to. Procreation pulls the plug out; the pool starts draining. It's a form of erosion. Children by nature eat your money, shred your time and gobble the best of your life. They say you never did anything for them and then they grow up and leave home and forget to write. Or worse yet, they don't leave, but hang around scattering crumbs like pollen, making it hard to breathe, expecting to be supported forever. That was my position.

Yet here I am, thoroughly immersed in the Toddler Lifestyle: emotional vulnerability not merely on a date but actually married to financial reality. How did it happen, this surrender into motherhood? Was it pure chance, just a fluke, my number coming up on the wheel of fortune, or was my bio-clock sending subliminal messages which could not be denied? Or does a third possibility exist, that this—this *parenting thing*—is just part and parcel of God's perfect plan for my life? In short, that my baby was predestined for my womb, and my role as a mother on this planet was simply meant to be?

Careful planning definitely had nothing to do with my decision to have a baby. Neither did the enticing lure of nine months *sans* PMS. I wasn't playing Russian roulette with our condoms and the rhythm method. My pregnancy wasn't planned. But it wasn't an accident either. It was something else entirely.

★★★★★

So how did I get here? Sounds like the title of a book I might take out of the library and read aloud to my kids, one squashed on either side of me, jammed up like puppies climbing over each other to reach the teat. Having a baby is more than a big change; it's a whole new life!

Children's books on reproduction tend to begin where the sperm meets the egg. In reality, it's hard to say where any story begins. I wouldn't have had children if I hadn't met Brian (or at least, I wouldn't have had *these* children); I wouldn't have met Brian if we hadn't been going to the same university; getting to university was but a link in a long chain which Brian's grandparents started when they immigrated from Japan around the turn of the century. (I don't know when my ancestors immigrated from Europe. I grew up on the same farm on the prairies that my great-grandparents lived on, and they came there from the East, not the Old Country.) No big miracles, no big surprises—just a string of events leading to a point.

At any rate, I found Brian bartending in the students' pub where I went with my fellow English literature majors for a couple of cold ones after grueling lectures on Dickens or Atwood. He had the most beautiful bone structure of any man I'd ever met and I've always been a sucker for black eyes and hair. I knew he was taking physics and math, so he had to be smart, and he moved with a quick, graceful precision behind the bar. He had beautiful hands. And that's about as much thought as I put into choosing the man who has turned out to be my life partner.

Coming from a long tradition of kind, gentle men as I do, I figured I had a knack for pickin' 'em sweet off the vine, but when Brian turned out to be witty and interesting, that was a bonus. He made me laugh and he appreciated the fact that I found him funny. He needed a lot of private space inside, but that was okay. If he wanted to be away from me, he just closed a door in his mind and he was gone.

Sharing an apartment was groovy, to say nothing of cheap, but I didn't want to get married. We pledged our eternal love to each other high in the branches of our favorite tree one night when the full moon made the huge green leaves so shiny they almost glittered. That was good enough for me. We kept our money separate. We spent Christmases apart.

University was the thing. It kept us very busy. I think I could have lived that way for a long, long time. But I didn't.

Brian and I were recovering from our fall semester's post-exam fight. We both tended to squirrel our anxiety away and barf it up at the first available break in the tension. Our predictable thing: my spotlight cameo, an irrational, emotional explosion, followed by Brian's part— angry, sulky silence for three or four days, during which time I took the minor role (regret and abject humility in the background). After that, we would have a reunion. We would go out, and drink heavily from sheer relief. This particular incident followed the usual pattern and we had reached reconciliation stage. Brian's best friend joined us and we all went downtown to get very silly on pitchers of cheap beer in a cheesy establishment which featured highly obnoxious music. Really, it didn't matter. Making up has its own high.

And so it was that we found ourselves walking home, Brian and I, late at night, tottering down residential sidewalks through the giant, moon-cast shadows of trees. It was as though we moved through a dark and silent garden. Surrounded by a black-hidden fecundity of green. December on the West Coast, wet and heavy in spite of the clear sky. All a-glow at the end of the evening, shrouded with the mist of our own breath, holding hands tightly against the cold edge on the air, star-kissed. Slid the key into the lock by moonlight, let each other in. The quiet waiting apartment, familiar, soothing. The abbreviated night routine (no one with contact lenses gets to just fall into bed). And then, finally, when we were where we most longed to be, between flannelette sheets with our arms around each other, safe and secure, I said to Brian, without giving the words coming out of my mouth a thought, "Betcha if we make love tonight, I'll get pregnant."

And *he* said, "Five bucks."

I was *so sure.*

★★★★★

I had chosen my apartment carefully for its location: the bus route to the university was good, my great-aunt Jean lived around the corner, I could walk downtown in ten minutes and, five blocks away, the ocean, with its rocky shore and driftwood, dependably provided a calming comfort and a place to throw stones.

So I didn't need a car. If you've never had one, you don't know what you're missing. The ultimate knack to living without personal transportation is that on those rare occasions when you really need wheels, you must remind yourself just how much insurance, gas and parking you haven't been paying recently and cheerfully call a cab.

I didn't. I woke up the next morning late for a post-exam dissection with some fellow English-major types and decided that, in spite of the time, it would be best for everyone if I got some fresh air.

I wasn't so much hung over as hung up. "Jo," I said to myself, "did you have to do that? You are truly irresponsible. Now you can spend your Christmas with your family in a state of anxiety. How charming!" and I quickly calculated when I could expect mental relief in the form of menstruation and when I should plan to panic, sighed deeply, and made the usual useless promises to conduct myself properly in the future.

When I got downtown I had a black coffee while I listened to my schoolmates discuss whether the exam on Chaucer was fair or even possible, and then I bought something cheap to fill my stomach, which was growling. I sat wedged in a booth at that crowded restaurant, sucking on my bottom lip and analyzing whether the uncomfortable stretched feeling sliding down the inside of my hip bones to my pubic hair was what I normally felt at that time of the month; alternatively I told myself to calm down and behave.

Women of childbearing age have been doing this routine since the beginning of time. It's the Individual against Survival of the Species here. Mrs. Brown, ninety years old and wheelchair-bound in the bachelor suite next to mine, told me over and over how she had had three children in three years and finally told her husband to stay away from her. He said, "Jeez, Mary, all I have to do is hang my pants on the door and you get pregnant." They didn't have another kid for five years and I bet I know how that was achieved too.

Don't bilge to me about the beauties of modern birth control either. Pretty little pink pills like cancer-causing candy, a blow-up balloon (but will he wear it?), a little rubberized Frisbee (Mom had one of those— and three of us), coils and crosses and baubles (if your womb will tolerate them). Go for it! Choose on! All the goodies are there. In the meantime, about three quarters of the women I know have had abortions. Kind of says something, wouldn't you say?

I had plenty of time to think things over. And believe me, I thought them over. I went home for Christmas and Brian went to his parents. My sister gave me *Howard's End*. I tried to quit smoking—something I always did when I went home, a habit not in the least conducive to having a relaxing visit. And while I socialized and did the Happy Noël thing, read my novels for the next semester and went for long walks in the glittering snow, I worried.

I worried because deep inside, I knew what was happening, even though my conscious mind was in revolt. I worried because I knew I could never have an abortion. I'd fight for pro-choice till my teeth fell out, but for me, it would never do. Most of all, I worried about the baby. What kind of life! Two starving students in a difficult world—how would we provide for it? What would we do? Poor little sod, with a mother who said she'd never have kids. I put myself through the wringer.

Finally, I'd had enough. I made myself quiet, and I had a wee chat with that baby—her/him/it. I told him that we wouldn't be able to give him everything, we didn't have a lot of money, nor the prospect of making much in the future; we didn't want a lot of things. I told him that this world's a mess, basically has been since Lucy the hominid fossilized in Africa; I mentioned urban crime, the ozone layer, the public-school system. "But," I said, "if you want to come, you're welcome!"

Then I opened my heart, and all the love I was afraid to show tumbled down like Rapunzel's hair, in a startling, surging, secret rush. Amazed, I hugged myself. Mentally, I let go. "Okay," I said, "if it's going to be, here's the space to let it be."

Anyway, that little speech got me through the month, without side effects, and that counts for something. Sometime in January I trotted off to the doctor, feeling quite stupid and paranoid actually, peed into a bottle and sat there alone, checking out her tools, waiting to be dismissed. I didn't know my doctor was going to give me "same day results," so I just about fell off my nasty little wooden chair when she came in smiling with a chunk of plastic in her paw and made her announcement: positive. Then she asked, was I okay with that?

"Oh, sure," I said nonchalantly, as though she was telling me she'd accidentally put relish on my plain burger. I staggered out of there an altered woman.

✶✶✶✶✶

And Brian?

Brian wanted kids—someday. That was a difference of opinion we had chosen to ignore. He thought forty would be a good age to start. During university, on the other hand, did not seem a propitious time to bring forth issue. In addition, the previous summer Brian had developed a back problem. By November it was so bad, he couldn't sit down. He regularly woke up at 3:00 AM in spasm and lay beside me groaning until dawn. He munched codeine like pretzels. He crept through the usual hoops, seeing the university doctor, the back specialist, and the surgeon's secretary in rotation.

I couldn't keep up with the diagnosis. The whole situation was one of the contributing factors in our pre-Christmas blow-up; I thought Brian should Do Something about his back. Anything. Including checking out the dazzling and prolific assortment of new-age alternative healing techniques advertised in the local magazines and on the billboards of all the good health-food stores. I thought he should meditate, learn pain control, amputate, join a support group. Brian thought if he waited it out, his back would get better. In some ways, he's a very patient, very stubborn man.

I thought God was testing me. I went about my business chanting, "This is not my problem, this is not my problem, this is not my problem." I would have controlled Brian if I could have, but he refused to be controlled.

When I met Brian in the university cafeteria for coffee that January and told him my big news, he was so overwhelmed that he sat down. It was the first time I'd seen him sit in months, a momentous occasion. Then he went to the pub, had too many beers and, to my great irritation, told all his buddies that he was going to be a papa. And then he came home and ate a pickle dipped in jam since we didn't have any ice cream.

Lentil Soup

(Cheap Food for Students)

Make a pot on Sunday and eat it for a week. That was my philosophy in university. Hey, if you get really ambitious, you can even heat it up.

Simmer
2 cups lentils (red or brown, both are equally nice) in water with a **bay leaf.** While the lentils are becoming soft, start chopping.
You will want
onions
garlic
celery
potato
carrot and any other vegetable you have sitting in your fridge.
Add
thyme, pepper and **salt.** When the lentils are soft, open a can of **tomatoes** (unless you have fresh ones), drain the juice into the soup and cut the tomatoes into pieces as you drop them in.
You will also need a
tablespoon of olive oil to make this soup really delicious.

Eat with brown bread to complete the protein.

When Sunday rolls around, make the same again, but with **mushrooms, basil** and **beef broth** instead of thyme and tomatoes.

Vary at will. It's cheap. It's nutritious. First complainer is the next meal's cook.

TWO

On the whole, Brian behaved pretty well. I hadn't really expected him to lose his cool in a big way. For one thing, he came from such a strong, upright, moral family: a family where men supported their children and did not abandon their wives (even common-law ones). Also, he was in many ways very passive. If he wanted to make a statement, he was more likely to make himself a dead weight than to throw a fit. There has been a fair bit of dead weight in our career as a couple, while *I've* thrown a fair number of fits. It evens out.

Looking back, I realize we were spared enormous financial anxiety because we weren't finished our degrees yet. You see, we both had staggering student loans coming due the moment we failed to provide proof of being full-time students. Baby or no baby, there seemed little point in quitting school so close to the end, without completing our degrees, so our mountain of debt was to remain background scenery for a little longer. The pain of payback time was postponed.

Meanwhile, Brian had a pretty good job bartending at a nightclub downtown and I worked off and on for my elderly great-aunt Jean. She was clinically blind. I did whatever she wanted me to do (reading, cleaning, writing), and then we chatted; she was a wonderful friend! When I told her I was pregnant, she said, "I thought you weren't going to do that," and then sent me out with money to buy a camera in anticipation of baby pictures.

My patched-up emergency idea was to finish my course work during pregnancy and take six months off after baby arrived, ostensibly to write my honors paper, the last big essay which would wrap up my university career. Then I figured I'd put the kid in daycare and go to work. That was the plan.

Not to say we were under any illusion about the usefulness of our degrees: Physics for Him, English for Her. I don't want you to think I was totally stupid. It's just that while an English degree is virtually useless, three quarters of a degree is even worse. What did we think we were doing, studying expensive and frivolous subjects while racking up loans? Well, Brian originally wanted to be a scientist, and I was indulging myself.

I had thought, "I was a secretary before. I can be a secretary again." I didn't intend to have a child to slow me down. And I didn't count on the world economic situation getting as bad as it did.

Yep, things really changed during the five years I was at university. When I arrived in 1986, the fresh-from-high-schoolers clamored loudly about "The things you gotta do to getta job," meaning higher education. By the time I graduated five years later, the first-years didn't talk about getting a job. University was just something to do while they waited to be unemployed some more. Depressing.

Anyway, there seemed little to do but buy vitamins and hunker down to study like a demon. Two surprises on that score, both physical. My body required more than vitamins as a result of my little parasite, and it rapidly became obvious that I wasn't going to be able to take six courses and be pregnant at the same time. I still wanted to graduate in the honors program (a matter of pride) so I needed a certain standard in my marks. But I couldn't stay awake!

People with children kept telling me, "It may be hard to get things done now, but after the baby arrives, it's gonna be so much worse. Just wait, there's no comparison." Maybe so, but those first three months, I just wanted to roll into a ball and hibernate. I wanted to lie on the futon in our bachelor suite with the venetian blinds slatted open and gaze out at the space between the parking lot and the top of my window frame where a strip of light filtered pale green through my neighbor's gigantic weeping willow. I wanted to contemplate each precious item in our crowded space, the green-and-gold handwoven cloth which my mother had brought back from Nigeria tacked over the open mouth of our closet, our books, my grandma's brown wicker chair with the blue woollen cushions donated by Aunt Jean, the vine we called Great Plant Racing Around the Room, the pitted hardwood floors, the peeling window sills.

I was content with it all. I was grateful not to be sick, but dreamy fatigue weighed every cell in my body. I wondered how women could possibly look after Child One when they were pregnant with Child Two. I wondered how Mrs. Brown had had three kids in three years, without allowing the older ones to drown in the creek while gestating the third. I did *not* wonder why there are so few women of child-bearing years in influential positions. No wonder women struggle on the corporate ladder. A couple of kids hanging from your pantyhose would definitely bang about the ankles some. And how many men spend two years of their prime career time with a terrible case of sleeping sickness? Minimum? Per child?

However, pregnancy had one physical fringe benefit for which I had not been prepared. To my delight, for the first time in my life, I was relieved of my existential angst! In spite of my public persona (habitual, perky cheerfulness), in private I have always suffered from "reason-for-being disease." You'd think my religion would have been a comfort, since I have dubiously believed in a spirit greater than ourselves for as long as I can remember. But then, so did the guy who wrote Ecclesiastes and he was the king of existential angst. Or at least the prince.

An assertive and strident part of me believes that life is so hard, painful and uncertain so much of the time, that it is absolutely crazy to keep on carrying on and caring. As though any of our measly little lives were important in the least! How much of what ties us and worries us will matter in ten years? Let alone a century. Yet we crawl along the surface of this earth, obsessed with our own insignificant existence.

After twenty-five years (yes, I was born this way) of listening to this kind of chit-chat buzzing around in my brain, I'd developed a paradox, a meditative tool similar to the *koans* which were used by Buddhist monks to help them move beyond reason toward intuitive enlighten-ment. "There are two truths to remember: Everything is intensely important, and nothing is important at all." It's perfect, don't you think? Sufficiently thought-provoking to provide a distraction if neces-sary, yet pithy enough to be used as a bandaid; so short it will fit in your purse or backpack, you can carry it everywhere; it slices, it dices—well, you get the picture.

But in my second month of pregnancy, I noticed I wasn't going through all that philosophical dither any more. I gave myself a little poke. Nope, no nihilistic discharge. Perhaps my own life lacked meaning in the grand scheme of things, but still, the new life inside me should have his or her chance! My whole body focussed on providing that, and my brain humbly followed along. And if there was anything incongruous about trotting along the biological treadmill in a world already over-populated and over-exploited by my species, my hormones were prepared to ignore the inconsistency. "Eat it!" I told my cosmic devils with glee. "I'm incubating!"

I couldn't believe how much I wanted my baby. It was as though this supposedly accidental conception had released the floodgate of desire and longing to have children that I'd kept back with practicalities and self abuse: *You're too broke to have kids, you're too flaky, you're too fringe, you're too unstable.* But with the deed already accomplished, I felt like Danae showered in gold. Br'er (or should I say Sister) Rabbit was deeee-lighted to be thrown in that Briar Patch!

I truly believed (and still do) that there is little you can do to get your mind ready for having a baby, outside of buying diapers. Nothing can alleviate the culture-shocking lifestyle change parenthood brings about. As for cultivating a moral climate, what you do not have within, you will do without, because children are so intuitive. They hear what we do, not what we say, and they're masters of subtext and manipulation. They absorb our ethics through the skin, from the moment of conception, and consume any discrepancy between belief and action along with the rest. It's scary, but liberating: there's little to do but stay true— as if that wasn't hard enough.

And obviously, I wasn't going to change the world just because I was pregnant. "Hey guys, I'm having a baby, so you just better smarten up. No more nuclear testing, and get that smutty crap off the TV. You there in the Middle East (to say nothing of Ireland and Bosnia), just get along, for crying out loud. I'm sorry, clear-cutting old-growth forests is just not acceptable, and all you happy shoppers out there, you've just got to stop buying over-packaged products. We've got enough garbage." Yeah, right, like even Hercules could fix the world in nine months and make it baby-safe.

I told myself cautiously, "Here's the reality, girl. You're having a baby. You're not going to be able to make the world nice for him overnight. The only thing to do is to take care of him or her the best you can for the rest of your life."

All this is not to say that I didn't consider abortion. One pretty much has to consider abortion, if only to the extent that the word blips across the mental screen. As for me, while I'd always maintained I would never have one, I was surprised to find it was on the list of options. I felt that to be responsible, I had to haul the concept out and have a good look at it. That intellectual activity influenced my attitude. Okay, we (and I choose the pronoun purposely) got pregnant in a moment of post-adolescent stupidity, but upon reflection, I chose to have the baby. (Again the pronoun fits. Brian's choice was "Accept my decision or walk out of our lives." Unfair, perhaps, but true.) I chose. I didn't have to have the baby. Nobody made me. I chose. I mentally reached inside and gave the fetus a little squeeze. Jest you 'n' me, gill-head.

I turned inward in a big way, perhaps because of the drowsiness, but partly because I'm an analytical person. Pregnancy gives new meaning to the term navel gazing. Here was scope to outdo any of my previous obsessions! Who was this person lodged inside my body, so familiar, yet so strange? I felt so close to that creature, mentally as well as physically, and I asked myself quite rudely and skeptically how that could be, having never met the child! Yet I was in love with all the passion of my being, and the ripples spread out in concentric circles to the very edges of my psychic pond. I felt close to Brian, since he and his parents and his grandparents were suddenly all in my belly at once. In fact, I'd suddenly doubled my genetic quantity, more or less, and I felt a jolting kinship with strangers on buses and streets. A fierce love surrounded me.

In my heart, I knew everything would be all right—much like life: sometimes hard, sometimes good. Much like life. In short, I was absolutely stoned on pregnancy.

Brian on the other hand was totally outward-focussed. He called the baby "Finn."

"Right, because he's swimming, huh?" I said. But no. Brian chose the name because "fin" is slang for a five-dollar bill. He paid up his bet-debt with the crispest money he could find and watched reverently as I put it in a file marked "Finn's Important Stuff." I could see Brian imagining his son looking through that file in the someday-future, rifling through the bits of paper, finding the money and asking about it. In fact, I could see Brian getting all warm and gooey. I took it as a good sign. That he could remember what it felt like to be a child. That he could picture himself as a dad.

Of course, Brian imagined a son. He was the youngest of three boys, and his brothers had five sons between them. Brian would have liked to have a girl, just to show up his brothers and make himself a kind of instant success to his parents, but he didn't really think it was going to happen.

The prospect of an actual baby seemed very distant and illusory to Brian. When they decide they want children, most people think of a cute little baby; very few plan to have a gangly, lippy, pimply adolescent, but Brian was more likely to discuss Finn as a teenager than the imminent arrival of another occupant in the apartment. He worried about being an appropriate role model for a boy, and fantasized about sending his son off to the football stadium alone, hot-dog money in one pocket, bus fare in the other. "I can't do that macho shit," he said. He also had a little skit which he would haul out and act for me about *Finn the Chartered Accountant.*

"Can I borrow the car?"

"No, Dad, not till you cut your hair."

Brian was interested in Finn's future but he wasn't obsessed, as I was. He could forget the future from time to time, as the present was trying enough. He would lose himself in his studies, in his preoccupation with work and always in trying to manage his chronic, grinding back pain.

And pregnancy, as a condition, didn't turn Brian on at all. He considered the fetus to be an alien. As such, I was an alien's hostess. While I was busy doing my cosmic-bonding thing, Brian was preparing for a green midget to spring from my massive gut and cry, "Take me to your leader." He didn't know how I could stand it.

We ate out. We probably shouldn't have done that. In fact, though I believed we were living fairly cheaply, we had not yet even begun to understand the meaning of the word frugal. But Brian believed life was not worth living if one could not eat out—a characteristic I admit I found absolutely endearing. Plus, we had this sense of impending doom as we perused menus hung in doorways downtown. Even the most well-behaved of children would doubtless change our role as patrons considerably.

And so we relaxed over steaming bowls of wor wonton: eleven different vegetables with bits of barbecued pork, shrimp and chicken floating around the noodles in a savory broth. We ate an entire condiment dish of chili paste between us with our soup. Or we'd go Japanese and have a big bowl of steaming clams, dripping with garlic and butter beside our tekka maki. That was a good choice because Brian could stand up at the sushi bar while he ate. His back wasn't getting any better.

Existential Cookies

I always find counting a good alternative to using a *koan,* and what better to count than poppy seeds?

Pre-heat the oven to 350°F and grease two baking sheets.

Then cream
1 cup butter and
1/2 cup white sugar
Add
2 eggs
Mix in the following:
2 cups of white flour (if you're going to sin, sin)
pinch salt
3 tablespoons poppy seeds
1 teaspoon vanilla (make it good vanilla, because you can really taste it)

Mold this dough into seedy little balls and squash them flat on the baking sheet with the bottom of a glass dipped in sugar. If you don't have glasses any old jar will do. These cookies bake fast, so watch it. Ten minutes or so will do the trick.

Remember, eating is a form of meditation, so take it slowly. So many poppy seeds, so little time. Oops! All gone!

THREE

Good thing I didn't have to cook much; I'd have burned myself for sure. I pottered back and forth in my galley kitchen, dangerous with a knife, easily distracted by the notes on my cupboards, which was where I kept any words of interest:

"If I'm not beautiful, you're not looking at me right." Jo.

"If you're going to spill, pour over the sink." Mom.

"Think of God not as a noun but as a verb." Len.

"I do not believe in beliefs. I believe with total conviction that there might be things which are possible or probable." Brian.

The counter was permanently stained by the previous occupants, undoubtedly including countless students who put their pots down without hot-mats (and probably ate right out of them). The western sun slid through the venetian blinds and landed with a splat on our tiny red table under the window. The front door couldn't be opened fully unless the oven door was closed and there was just room to walk single file between the sink and counter and the table into the room where we read and slept.

I'd drift over to the futon, like some medieval lady in a trance, and recline. I couldn't believe the pull of gravity, the Earth whispering, "Come to me, come to me," the huge urge to just lie down. I used every ounce of energy I had just to get to classes and keep my eyelids open. If I floated around in a dream state, well, so be it, I told myself, as long as I got my essays in and managed to visit the doctor at the appropriate times.

Going to the doctor is what you do when you are pregnant. When I complained about it, my doctor coolly informed me that Canada has the lowest rate of infant mortality in the world, so I hunkered down in my home away from home, the doctor's waiting room.

My old doctor didn't deliver.

"What do you mean, you don't deliver?" I whined. I liked my doctor. I didn't want a new one. I had to get a new one anyway.

The first time I went to see the new doctor, she told me to go and buy a book on pregnancy and parenting. I was so annoyed that I strode straight to the nearest bookstore and dropped $20 on *Anna Karenina* in paperback, plus a spanking-new copy of *Where the Wild Things Are*. Clearly, one could not parent without the latter. I figured people have been having babies more or less successfully for years without the benefit of self-help books, and if I had a problem I'd call my sister, who is my idol, and knows everything.

I did stop at the drugstore and pick up a free copy of *Best Babies*, which was put out by the government. It was pretty good. What I remember best was that I was advised to get a bed ready for the baby, even if it was only a cardboard box. I found that reassuring—it reminded me of my mother's story about sleeping in the bottom drawer of the bureau. She was a Depression baby. If she grew up without money or Fisher Price toys, surely so could Finn.

Then I went to the library and got out a kids' book with dazzling photography of cells dividing and little seahorse, peanut-headed creatures floating around in amniotic fluid.

About the eleventh week the doctor heard Finn's heartbeat. I made Brian come to my next appointment. The doctor handed him the earphones plugged into her little black box, and Brian's black head bent over my huge white sea of belly to hear our baby's speedy, secret heartbeat sloshing "Whoop, whoop, whoop." I heaved myself upright and we came out into the sunny street, blinking.

"Well," said Brian heavily, "we'd better go buy a mobile."

As I said, Brian had a problem with even the concept of a newborn baby. By the time we got to the Science and Nature Store, he had recovered. I bought a mobile. Brian bought a paper falcon with nine hundred and seventy six individual pieces. He still hasn't put it together yet. In fact, I have it in the file marked "Finn's Important Stuff," along with his hospital bracelet and the lovely new five-dollar bill.

My belly was outrageous. I had always imagined that would bother me. I love my body. It's lean and compact and it does what I want it to do. Not a sports model, but nice lines, good mileage, low maintenance and repair. Although good looks are great, let's face it: you can buy 'em if you really want 'em; comfort comes first. Maybe I didn't mind my new role as Hippo Woman because I wasn't really uncomfortable.

I'd sit in the literary theory class I was taking, rubbing my belly as if it were a Buddha charm, trying to make sense of deconstructionalism and post-structuralism. I really wanted to remember what I learned in that class. Such scope for pretentiousness. Imagine discussing Derrida in the delivery room! "You getting this, Finn?" I'd ask. I thought I was going to have the best-educated baby in Canada. I was counting on my second brain to give me an added edge at exam time.

You know what I liked best? Riding the bus. Sitting in my favorite seat at the back with my book bag at my feet, holding my belly and communing with my baby. I thought, does everyone feel like this when they're pregnant? I thought, with so much love, how could anything go wrong? I'd look at the people and think, "Did your mama feel this way about you?" Those great clumsy lumps, men in suits, teenagers in those super-baggy pants, boxer shorts and chains on their wallets, shit-kicking boots. Women with painted-on masks, sweet-faced girls, mean-faced girls, the boy with the violin and the man with the pony-tail, all those people, did their mothers hold their bellies and worship them *in utero*?

It occurred to me that any one of those people (who knew which) could be rich, rich in their own secret halo of love. And I felt a stab of pain to think that of course, plenty of those people didn't have that gift. There are plenty of unwanted pregnancies, and lots of women too busy to even think about their bellies. At the time, this seemed to me a huge denial of the individual's greatest right—both the mother's and the child's.

Brian, on the other hand, worried about the baby being deformed. He wasn't sure he could cope with a normal baby, let alone the added stress of a special-needs child. Then one night, he dreamed that our baby was completely misshapen, but he put out his arms and held the child, and to his profound relief, felt unconditional love.

That was a great moment, although the dream brought another revelation with it. Brian said he'd been thinking that everything would be okay when we saw that the baby was born healthy. In the dream he realized birth is only the beginning. Finn could get sick, or be run over by a bus. We would never be free from worry again.

"Unless of course Finn dies," I said cheerfully.

"Or we die," added Brian, and then we both laughed. Imagining the worst was one of the ways we made the present feel safe. We turned fear into a bonding thing.

As my belly got bigger, the public took over ownership. I wonder if that phenomenon is a hangover from the long-ago days when we actually did live in community? Or are we just starved, as a culture, for small children and animals in our lives? Anyway, I could not buy groceries or take a book out of the library without discussing my due date with a total stranger. And what really surprised me was the Icky Pregnancy Stories.

"My sister's best friend Harriet had a baby and he was born with a cleft palate. The cord got stuck in his lip and they both died."

"My friend's baby is a hermaphrodite Siamese twin. They're waiting to see which sex is dominant and then they're going to operate."

"A fungus grew in my cousin's womb. It covered the baby's face and it smothered."

It happened over and over again. People just could not resist. Incredibly gruesome or morbid stories, ranging from fetuses ripped from the womb by psychopathic necrophiliac pedophiles to weird and devastating unusual diseases to ninety-hour labors. The tendency to tell this stuff was so unbelievably pronounced that I wasn't upset as much as mesmerized. What a weird thing to do! Or was it just a variation on the Worst Case Scenario game Brian and I played. The *Best Babies* handbook didn't prepare me for this.

Prenatal classes didn't help me on that score either. Yes, we went. Chiefly I wanted to learn how to breathe so I didn't suffer in labor. And I did learn breathing, but I'm not sure that it was a net gain. I'd never been in a room with so many pregnant yuppies in all my life. Being a woman with a very liberal smattering of personal insecurity, I prefer to feel at a disadvantage in small doses.

In my better moments, I think of myself as an interesting and thoughtful person, who tries as far as possible to live life in a moral way. At the very least, my mama loves me! But let's face it. Our society puts a high value on money, status and power. Here we were, Brian and I, barefoot and pregnant, living in a bachelor suite in a building so old the tile peeled off the floor in the bathroom and the ghost of Marilyn Monroe lived in the toilet, causing it to gurgle in a helpless, quiet way and sometimes overflow with no provocation (poor Marilyn)—here we were in a room full of fat women, discussing the color schemes in their nurseries.

It brought out the worst in me. We divided into little groups; we were supposed to come up with some of our concerns about pregnancy. After a long discussion about stretch marks, someone mentioned being afraid of labor.

"What's to be afraid of?" I quipped. "You're either going to have a baby, or they'll give you a Caesarean, or you'll die."

Nobody laughed. If I'd been more with it, I'd have asked them if absolute strangers told them Icky Pregnancy Stories too. Maybe it was something about me, personally, that attracted that kind of thing.

Dear me. I had real trouble seeing myself as part of an established married couple with a bouncing little bundle of joy on the way. When I look back, there was no way that group could have been as homogeneous as I made it out to be, but I become unfair when I'm intimidated, and I don't like groups at the best of times.

We did pick up some useful information at prenatals. And there was a spin-off benefit: all those shirts reminded me how lucky I was to have Brian, who will never, ever, ever be a shirt. Shirts do not save a little queue of hair at the nape of their necks, braid it and grow it to their bums. A shirt would never say, "I am not from this planet. I am here as a punishment for an intergalactic parking misdemeanor." Or recite "To be or not to be" the first time he walks you home. These were things I found extremely charming, along with more substantial qualities like fidelity, integrity, 20/20 vision and the kind of skin pigment rarely seen in cancer patients.

Kabucha Bread

Amazing what comes in the package deal when you get a partner, baggage that never occurs to you while you're checking out the fit of his jeans. The stuffed bear from his childhood, the Attitude, the relatives— it all comes with the guy.

I found this recipe in Brian's family-reunion cookbook. Me, I'm just looking for a good way to disguise squash. All that vitamin A. Have to get it down somehow.

Preheat the oven to 350°F. Blend:
1 cup white sugar
1/2 cup brown sugar
1/2 cup vegetable oil
1 cup cooked, mashed squash

Now, I'm sorry, but you will have to think. Or intuit. Whichever works best for you in the kitchen. If the squash is the really dry kind, you need to add
1/4 cup water. However, if it's a really juicy butternut squash or even pumpkin, the water should be left out.

Now do the dry ingredients:
1 cup white flour
1 cup brown flour
1 teaspoon baking soda
1/4 teaspoon salt
1/2 teaspoon each nutmeg, cinnamon, ginger

Add the drys to the wets and mix. If you like, stir in
raisins and/or nuts

Bake in a well-greased loaf pan for 60 to 70 minutes, or until done (you know, the toothpick comes out clean and nice cracks are starting to form on top).

Remove from the pan and cool. Feed to unsuspecting pregnant women and small children.

FOUR

After a while, I began to feel like I'd been pregnant forever. I forgot there was a time when my body was my own, to use and abuse without consideration for another creature. At the same time, I was aware that my life was going to change even more: that we, baby and I, would no longer be a self-contained unit, and the baby was going to be extremely demanding.

One Sunday afternoon Brian and a couple of his old-time buddies went pub crawling. I stayed home finishing schoolwork, but when he called me later in the evening, I took a cab and went downtown to join him—just because I could. That much of my life was still my own; maybe I couldn't have a drink, but I could still leave the house as a single unit. I didn't have to get a baby-sitter.

I'm glad I had that awareness. I'm glad I had the sense to appreciate those last few months when I could just pick up and do nearly whatever I wanted. I'm glad I spent a lot of time curled up, reading, eating veggies dipped in yogurt and onion soup mix or dill, or hot buttery toasted tomato sandwiches, or crackers and cheese. I slept whenever I wanted to. I went for long walks.

One twilight, our building caretaker and friend, John, asked me if I'd seen the moon. "It's almost as big as your belly." He walked me down to the ocean to watch that big fat globe float over the water. The blossoms made the narrow residential streets into a cathedral and we walked from between them onto the shore. The water stretched shimmering out to the mountains like the rainbow road to fairy heaven. Ocean, rocks, moon and softening light. Oh, my baby. Welcome! Blessings: water, earth, sky. Too bad we didn't have fire too, but nothing's perfect.

★★★★★

Brian picked out names. Naming, as a hobby, is right up my alley (significant words and all) so I really surprised myself when I released that honor to Brian. But you see, I already felt so connected to the baby that I had no need to strengthen my bond. Brian didn't feel that way. He wasn't getting the same biological encouragement that I was. In fact, baby and I were in a secret world he couldn't really enter, so giving the naming to him (and especially choosing to call the baby by Brian's last name) was a serious gesture for me, an invitation to an exclusive club. An acknowledgment of importance, a toast to the expectation that Brian would be there with us, always.

Mind you, I could have exercised my veto rights if Brian hadn't picked well. He chose traditional Japanese names, although his actual working knowledge of Japanese was limited to what he had ignored during the hated private lessons of his childhood and all that he could absorb in two years of language classes wedged in between his science courses at university. Ethnic names were a perfect choice in my opinion because I wanted something unusual, but not too bizarre like "Canadian-Summer" or "Cinnamon Pop-cycle."

I was so fortunate. I loved being pregnant, I loved that closeness to the baby. I had very little physical discomfort and, while I worried a lot about what we were going to do for money, nothing bad actually happened. Still, by August I wanted my body back. I have a theory (which does not work at all for preemie babies) about Hotel Womb: *Perfect Union, Total Care.* It is so comfortable that a baby will not leave until the mother has reached her absolute maximum tolerance and is ready to scratch a hole in her belly with her fingernails.

And people are so awful! "Haven't you had that baby yet?" Lay off, I changed my mind, I'm not going to have it, alright? A girlfriend of mine, two weeks overdue, said she'd decided to become a hood ornament—just sit up there on the front of a fancy car and grow like a pumpkin. I saw one woman downtown, with more nerve than I'll ever have, hugely pregnant in a T-shirt that read, "What the fuck you staring at?"

To go with that, I remember writing to my sister about a story that was printed in our local rag, about a pregnant woman who ordered a daiquiri to go with her meal. Her waiter refused to bring her the drink—even hauled out the federal warning label from a bottle of beer and read it to her. "Drinking alcohol while pregnant could be dangerous to the fetus."

Apparently the woman was two weeks overdue. "This baby had his chance to be born alcohol-free!" she screamed at the manager, who fired the offending waiter. I loved it: just the thought of that woman, arms akimbo in the only remaining dress that could possibly fit, a muumuu, garish and loud, frizzy hair flying, feet planted firmly for balance, fists clenched, causing a scene in the middle of a sophisticated restaurant. "Give me my daiquiri!" Very pregnant women are not civilized.

Or how about this one, that Aunt Jean told me: apparently hospitals in the 1920s weren't what they are now, and my aunt was bunked up next to some other woman in the throes of labor. This woman was flat on her back, in a most undignified position, and the doctor came in to take a look: all pompous, surveying his kingdom, hands behind his back, complete with subservient nurse three paces behind him. He made the mistake of coming too close. Aunt Jean's neighbor sucked back and kicked him—oooof!—right in the pot belly. The doctor lost his balance, hairpiece and glasses went flying, stethoscope snapped up and popped him in the nose, and he landed on his butt. He lost his composure entirely, got up spluttering and indignant.

"Why'd you do that?!"

And our friend on the cot snarled, "Because I *wanted* to!"

Oh yes!

By the end of pregnancy, one is just so fat, and so full, and so fed up, one just wants to kick like a swimmer. For some reason, in between the stage of nubile young thing and Madonna, there is a short and reassuring period where the crone rules, where woman finds herself cranky, irritable, undiplomatic, loud and rude. Comforting to know that under all that feminine softness, all that extra water lodging in your ankles, all that fat (*all* dedicated to this *growth* within you), there remains a hard and solid core which screams out, "Me! What about *me!!!*"

The closer we got to my due date, the greater swelled my sense of urgency to get things done. I was so relieved when I finished my last summer course. Then I was overcome by a violent desire to buy shelves. I went downtown with my little plastic trouble-making charge card in hand and bought a huge pine wall unit, the ladder-and-board kind that comes apart when you have to move. I paid to have it delivered and spent a whole night assembling it, all by myself. (Brian was at work and I couldn't wait.) Which was a feat. My upstairs neighbor must have been annoyed, but she was far too polite to mention it.

The biggest stresser was Brian's back. He'd finally decided that he wanted to be able to pick up his child and it was obvious he couldn't do that unless something changed, and it hadn't for eight months. He signed up for an operation. And wouldn't you know it? Our due dates were the same.

Now, let me just make myself clear here, if I can do that without being too vindictive. Here I was at a time when I felt that I (and my appendage) deserved to be the focus of attention and care. And here was Brian, clearly much worse off than I was, with an operation scheduled for the day I was supposed to pop—oh great! Brian, for a whole host of reasons, was not looking forward to being sliced open. And I—I wanted him to be there, with and for me, in the delivery room.

Before the baby came, labor loomed like this big event. I mean, there's a real sisterhood thing centered around labor stories. Before you have a baby, labor is the big initiation. Are you going to home birth or do the hospital route? Where do you stand on *the drug issue*? What's it going to be like? Of course, not so very many years ago, women died in labor; infants did too, so naturally the whole event was shrouded with vestiges of doom as well as anticipation of joy.

However, in our present-day culture, we've focussed on the physically painful event which detracts from the bigger, more permanent issue: *your life is about to be infiltrated and taken over completely!!!* Yes, labor can be truly horrible, but there's a maximum to how long it is going to last. But once you let a baby into your life, chances are it will be years before you get a solid night's sleep, and you will not so much as brush your teeth alone until your youngest child reaches the age of five. Many women agree with me on this. "Labor, labor, what is that?! It's like worrying about stubbing your toe as you fall into the lion's den."

But I fell for it just like everyone else. I was focussed on the labor thing, and here was Brian having this operation. My mom was coming out a few days before my due date. She didn't want me sleeping alone while Brian was in the hospital. Brian's parents planned to drive over in their RV. While we waited for our respective in-laws to rally around us, we were pretty glum. I was fat, Brian was in pain, and we were both scared.

And yet, of all my memories, this is one of the sweetest. University hadn't started yet. We were between projects. We holed up. Closed the blinds. Cuddled into bed, bolstered by a host of teddy bears, Brian with his pain-killers and I with my many pillows supporting all the parts of me that drooped (oh my poor loose joints!). He and I against the world, just we two.

We ate comfort food, which for Brian meant noodles. Kinky ramen steaming in deep bowls, with a dash of Louisiana hot sauce. Spaghetti with the thick, meaty, tomato sauce Brian taught me to spike with white wine and nutmeg, sprinkled with grated parmesan. Onions sautéed in olive oil and basil, with fresh chopped tomatoes and salt added at the last minute over flat egg noodles. Fast, delicious food. And I read aloud: *The Object of My Affection,* one of my all-time favorite books. Chapter after chapter till we lost track of time.

That could never happen in my present life. Someone would wake up and want Mama.

It was fabulous!

Stroganoff

(Another Noodle Comfort Food)

Just how comforting this is depends on whether you decide to attend to your fat intake. If you don't care, go for the following:
Sauté thin slices of
beef in
oil or butter. I prefer a good-sized steak which will slice up very fine when partially frozen. When the beef is almost done add thinly sliced
onions and
mushrooms. Use lots. Let all this simmer nicely together.
While the beef is bubbling, mix up about
1 tablespoon flour
1 tablespoon Dijon mustard
salt
pepper
1/4 teaspoon nutmeg and
1/4 cup stock or water in a shaker jar. If you have freshly grated nutmeg and pepper, so much the better. Stir the contents of the shaker jar in with the meat and see how it looks. You can thin it out with more stock or water if you wish, depending on how soupy you like your stroganoff sauce to be. However, make sure this mixture bubbles long enough to cook the flour.
Then add
1/4 cup white wine and
1 cup sour cream. Stir. Let it heat nicely without boiling, and it's ready to eat over noodles.
If you are watching your fat, or you're a vegetarian, comfort yourself by substituting chickpeas for the beef. In this case, sauté the onions and mushrooms first, using a little butter or simmer them in a little stock or water if you're really pure. Then add the cooked
chickpeas, and proceed with the recipe.
When you get to the sour cream part, whip out your container of
low fat yogurt and carry on.

This method combines flavor with virtue, should you find that kind of thing comforting.

FIVE

Mom drove out as planned and stayed with me in the apartment while Brian had his operation, right on schedule. Thank God for Medicare. Mom took me out to see him at the hospital the next day— limp in bed, Mr. Demerol Head. He was a pretty pathetic sight. Zapped by the hospital colors, visual pablum. Brian's dad raises chrysanthemums; great blossoms, gorgeous, so huge that it's hard to comprehend that they're real. Brian had a five-gallon bucket of them on his table, the only color in the room. There was nothing for him to do but wait out the pain. Some of his co-workers came by to play chess, which I can only assume was a help.

I went into labor in the night. Mom woke up and asked me if I was okay, and I said I didn't feel well. I thought I was getting the flu. She told me to go back to sleep and so I did. When I woke up again at 6:00, my situation was a little more obvious. Mom was more excited than I was. She wanted to time my contractions, which were still minuscule. She also wanted to get me out to the hospital, which is quite a long drive out of town. We left a note on my in-laws' van saying where we were and drove off.

I didn't want to check into the hospital until I had to, but I went up to the third floor to see Brian and tell him our big news.

"We're having a baby today!" He gave me his big eyes, all soft, and squeezed my hand.

"Does it hurt?"

"Not yet," I told him, and went back outside to walk around the hospital parking lot for about six hours. It's quite beautiful there, lots of trees and green. Not your usual cement wasteland. But still, it was a long time to hang out. Periodically I'd check in with my Significant Other. The doctor had told Brian he could come up to the delivery room for the crucial moment, so he was saving up his drugs.

Everyone has their own special labor. Mine wasn't too bad, as far as labors go. I checked into the hospital in the afternoon, before the pain got unreasonable. Mary, a girlfriend of mine who worked at the hospital, came and sat with me after she booked off work at about 4:30. By that time, Mom didn't want to be with me. She didn't want to watch me hurt. I had an enema and feces spurted from my bowels. I threw up vigorously and when I looked in the mirror it was a surprise to find that no blood jetted from my ears.

They had told us at prenatals that taking a shower would be relaxing and help the baby come faster. I sat on the bench in the stall with the water beaming down over me and rhythmically slammed my head against the wall. "This is ridiculous!" I groaned. "I'm never having another baby!"

I ordered up some drugs, but before they pushed the syringe in, someone near my nether parts announced that the baby was coming. I thought, "Right on. Now it will get better."

It didn't. They told me I could push. I pushed forever and each effort was like trying to drive a dinner knife into my flesh. Blunt, brutal pain.

"Good girl," they said, "we can see the head," like I was supposed to be pleased with this.

"Does it have any hair?" I wailed.

"Yes, there's lots of black hair."

"Is there enough to pull it out?" I heard someone guffaw, but I couldn't say who it was. I didn't have my contacts on, and, peevishly, I didn't want my glasses.

Perhaps it was just as well that I couldn't see, as there were a zillion people in the room. You'd think a woman would be offended, bare butt on a raised bed, groaning like a stuck pig, with more attendants than Queen Vicky—I did not give a shit. Mary was there, telling me I was doing a great job, plus a nurse, a doctor, and an intern. Then there was a specialist—I found out later that Finn had excreted feces in the womb, so a man stood by waiting to suction my baby's every crevice as soon as possible. My mother and in-laws were in the corridor, listening to me howl. (My mother-in-law and I discussed this later. She said I screamed. I said I didn't scream, I grunted loudly.) To top it all off, a photography student showed up and asked if it was okay to take pictures. "Do whatever the fuck you want!" I screamed.

Then Brian arrived, looking like a Saturday-morning cartoon of himself, with major bed-head, wrapped in a bathrobe. He was absolutely zoned on Demerol.

"Where's the ice chips?" he kept saying—appropriate for a bartender, wouldn't you say? He told me afterwards he had trouble reconciling the cute little pastel animals on the walls of the delivery ward with the medieval-torture-chamber shrieks echoing in the hallways.

When I finally popped that baby, I was so relieved that I didn't question that they whisked him away for suctioning; the doctors kept me busy pushing out the placenta. I didn't even ask what sex my baby was.

Brian hobbled over and said, "It's a Hiroshi." Hiroshi. A son. It took me a moment to compute.

Then I howled, "Give me my baby now!" and there he was in my arms, oh my god, oh my god, oh my god.

How can I possibly describe that moment, when I looked into my baby's face for the very first time? We have pictures; other people have pictures of their first moments too. Someone always manages to point the camera. These photographs (frequently blurry) feature fat, flushed women with bundles of swaddling in their arms. A tiny primate face beside which the mother's skin looks coarse.

In these pictures no angels sing. No heavenly host hosannas in the background. No halos glow. No ray of light descends like a beacon to herald the momentous event: a heart explodes here today! But between the whirlwind of hormones, the sweat and the pain in addition to nine months of anticipation, the moment when I first held my infant in my arms was without a doubt one of the most emotional in my life. Oh blessed baby, oh most exquisite child: hello.

Pregnant women were standing in line for my room, so I whipped right out of there. It was late, all my relatives went quietly home. Brian had long since been wheeled to the elevator upright on a trolley like a statue. The nurses put my son in the nursery and told me to get some sleep. I couldn't. I buzzed. It was the first time I'd been apart from that baby in forty weeks. I'd waited so long for him to be in my arms, I wanted to hold him, see him, breathe in his sweet private smell.

I didn't know we were permitted to have our babies in our rooms, so I crept into the nursery and found my husband's name on the bottom of a baby box. My bundle of swaddling clothes, my bundle with black fuzz for hair and a shriveled pink face. I found a rocking chair in a quiet corner and my son latched onto my breast like a suction cup.

"Good," I thought, "I don't have to teach you to eat. Fill your belly, dear one."

I rocked him all night long.

Celebration Gingercake

There are times in almost every woman's life when she wants to celebrate, she *deserves* to celebrate, but—there's this little matter of about five extra pounds. Or, if you've just had a baby, feel free to make that fifty pounds. Sigh. I must admit that while I enjoyed being pregnant, it was a very unpleasant surprise to discover that it takes months, sometimes even years, to get back into your jeans again. You might not even have much extra weight, but there's this redistribution problem . . .

Very well I remember the day that I phoned everyone I knew, even mere acquaintances, to tell them I had zipped my pants up.

So here goes. Applesauce gingercake. The trick is to replace most of the shortening with applesauce, thus eliminating countless calories (trillions, I'm sure), and you can use this trick in any recipe any time you feel adventurous. Or fat.

Set the oven to 325°F. Wets to drys, as usual. Mix:
1 1/4 cup applesauce
1/4 cup oil
1 cup molasses (blackstrap—it has more vitamins)
2 eggs
2/3 cup sugar
Also mix:
1 1/2 cup white flour
1 cup brown flour
2 1/2 teaspoons baking soda
1 teaspoon each ginger, cinnamon, and **allspice. Nutmeg** is also good.

Combine, but don't over mix. Pour in a greased 9" x 13" pan. Bake for a little over 30 minutes, checking carefully for signs of the cake pulling away from the pan and cracks on top. Try not to over cook.

And eat it hot.

SIX

A lot of women talk about the misery of the first three post-natal months. For a lot of women, the First Big Surprise of parenthood comes right on the heels of the drive home from the hospital. "Oh my *God*, I didn't know it would be like *this!*" That happened to my sister. She was under the impression that babies slept. She was under the illusion that she would be able to control her baby. She was the kind of person who'd ask, on airplanes or buses, "Why don't they keep that kid quiet?" Having her own baby was a terrible, terrible shock. She and her husband nicknamed her "Princess of Power."

From a lengthy list of parental pitfalls, each family finds their own personal pothole to sleep in, custom-designed for bad posture. There is colic—and if your baby has colic, you *all* have colic. I have heard terrible stories about perfectly healthy babies who screamed non-stop for the first three or four months.

And there is the isolation, which especially affects career women. After your friends bring the obligatory baby present over, coo at the infant and walk out the door, think, "Goodbye!" because career women are busy at work during the day. They have a life and don't understand why you don't any more. They don't realize that you need to be in bed by ten! If they have kids of their own, they don't have a life and couldn't fit you in without a six-month prior booking. A new mother can be stuck at home in a fortress surrounded by invisible barriers. Kind of like Atlas. You've got all the time in the world, but no free hands, and there's nowhere to go.

And of course, there's the sleeping thing. Another blooper I made at prenatals: my offering to the list of "Concerns about Parenting" was that I was afraid I'd never get to sleep again. My peers looked at me in stupefied silence.

Finally someone piped up, "Oh, you mean, like, if the baby is sick or something?"

"No," I said, "I mean, like, if the baby is *alive.*"

My cousin's baby only slept in twenty-minute stretches. My cousin was barely functional for five whole months.

Which only leaves me wondering not why infant abuse occurs, but why it doesn't occur more often. I've heard friends say that nothing, but *nothing*, prepares you for parenthood—you might as well try to prepare for being a paraplegic.

Myself, I expected the worst. I thought having a baby was going to be like baby-sitting, except that you could never give the baby back. I liked baby-sitting, baby-sitting was okay; but the absolutely essential ingredient was giving the baby back. I thought, therefore, that to tolerate an eighteen-year stretch of baby-sitting, I would probably require heavy sedation. I thought the way to do it was just to plow through, one day at a time, Valium vial in one hand and bottle in the other, and book a space in a detox center for twenty years down the road.

I didn't know about nature's own sedative, the chemical bio-rush that some very, very fortunate women get when their milk comes in, which prevents new mothers from throwing their children out the window. Having my own baby was not in the least like baby-sitting. I had much more tolerance for my own child.

And while intellectually I was quite aware that every parent thinks her own child is special, emotionally I firmly believed Hiro was the center of the universe, and there never was nor ever would be another child his equal. No wonder Mary was not surprised when the wise men bowed down to Jesus. Obviously, it was only fitting that they should. I felt quietly sorry for everyone who didn't have a baby, more specifically my baby.

My own first month was utterly beautiful. I gave myself permission to take a real break, and all I did was sit in the rocking chair holding Hiro to the breast with one arm, and propping my book open with the other. Every now and then I'd look down at that beautiful, clear little face, give a deep sigh of pleasure and go back to Wilkie Collins. The apartment gathered dust and mold. When I took my daily walk, I put Hiro in the Snugli (a wonderful device that strapped my baby to my belly like a little koala) and ventured out into autumn sunlight, greens and golds. I collected the finest of the glossy rich chestnuts, called conkers-bonkers by children for generations, and thought of how a small boy would be big enough to play with them soon.

I shopped every day at "the village" four blocks away, showing off Hiro's progress shamelessly to the checkout girls at my grocery store. I bought small quantities of vegetables and made simple, low-maintenance food like roast chicken, with baked potatoes and carrots on the side. If I only used one pot, I only had to wash one pot—so much the better!

Brian and I obsessed about Hiro's health, and worried ridiculously if he so much as whimpered.

"I feel so guilty bringing him into this world if he's not going to be happy," said Brian.

I still tended to feel Hiro was lucky to be alive at all, but fussed along with my better half. Was my son too warm? Maybe he was too cold. Was he running a temperature? Was he sleeping too much? Shouldn't the cord be off by now? Was he getting enough to eat? Meanwhile, I was making so much milk that I had to wear a double diaper wrapped around my chest to keep from soaking my bed at night. You'd think that would be a clue that the boy had enough to eat.

Brian, being of a scientific bent, made a complicated graph of all the variables, complete with temperature recorded every fifteen minutes on a normal day. Yet still we were not able to contain and control that life force. We could not beg, borrow, or steal the security that Hiro would be okay, forever and ever, no matter what. Eventually we had to resign ourselves to the inevitable—our son was on this Earth for the ride, both up and down, just like the rest of us. Luckily, for the most part his health was good.

A new baby doesn't stay a new baby very long. Within six weeks they go from helpless blobs to little E.T. creatures that will smile back at you. In fact, my most powerful emotion at that period of my life was the feeling that precious time was going by too fast. I wanted to save the minutes—I took a lot of pictures, trying to hold on to what I was feeling. I wanted to remember how Hiro lay there, fat with sleep, breathing from his belly, how his cheeks puffed up from lying on his face, the line from his eyebrow to his lip mirroring the wrinkle of his cotton sheet, and how he stretched his little legs as he woke up.

I wanted to eat it all up, like cream-filled croissants and jam—to taste every sip, like expensive coffee; yet each feeding, though sweet, was indistinguishable from the next. It seemed to me that I had scarcely said, "Hello," to my new son, before I was having to say "Goodbye" because he grew and changed so fast. As Brian said a little later in the year, "I can't wait until he starts walking, but oh! it will be so sad!" I knew exactly what he meant.

I think this afterbite of sadness was partially related to my father's death. We were very close, my dad and I, and when he died, I was an extremely immature eighteen-year-old. I hadn't passed the stage of idolizing him yet. I had graduated from high school and was hanging about the farm in between returning from a trip to Mexico (where I didn't learn Spanish, or at least not much) and looking for work. I had no idea what I was going to do with my life.

Dad slipped and knocked himself out when he was loading grain. It poured over him, and he suffocated before he had a chance to come to. That morning, he had waved at me across the yard. A whole-body activity, it was, his arms and legs splayed in a huge jumping jack in the snow. Just for me. Because he loved me. Because his enthusiasm spilled into even the smallest thing he did.

That afternoon he was dead, without so much as a goodbye.

There is nothing like death to illustrate this: when someone dies, they are really gone. They don't come back in the flesh to hold you. All their opinions and jokes get old. Death is the end of all new stories. If your relationship with a dead person needs healing, you must heal it on your own. So, like a vein of chocolate running through a white cake, my father's death is always with me, influencing the flavor of my life, bittersweet. After the first ten years, most of the pain is gone—what is left is the reminder of how precious time is, and the bite: never forget, this could all be taken away, could disappear forever, in an instant. Of this, I have living (or should I say "dead") proof.

So as Hiro changed with the typical speed of a healthy boy, it seemed to me that an integral part of my psychic life was telescoped, and I was witnessing a series of mini-births and mini-deaths. This was a gentler lesson in change than my father's abrupt and untimely demise, for of course I wanted my boy to grow. It was good and natural that he should, and the triumph and pleasure with which we greeted each new development sweetened the farewell to each passing phase. And yet—I felt as though an over-eager waiter was whisking away the last, delicious morsels of my meal before I had eaten my fill. To Brian's horror, I began talking about wanting another baby.

★★★★★

Brian and I were not having parallel experiences, to be sure! As well as recovering from back surgery, he didn't come from a family with a particular affinity for newborns, and, let's face it!—he had no tits. We'd been told that I should express milk so that Hiro would become accustomed to bottle feeding right from the start. Right from the start, Hiro was not interested. Mama or nothing. So from the start, we did not have "equal and shared parenting."

To my distress, Brian told me that he felt left out—that the baby was "my bag." I felt all the more guilty because, in my heart, I knew that if I had to choose between them, my baby would come first a thousand times. One of my friends told me that she thought she'd always love her husband best, since she had had him longest. However, after her daughter was born, she knew that what had passed for love before had been like those pretty, toy rings she chose after dentist appointments when she was a little girl, compared to the fierce, diamond love that she felt for her newborn child. Always super-intuitive, Brian was, as usual, right on the mark. He *was* left out. Much as I tried to include him, it was "baby and me" in my heart.

Brian remembers Hiro crying a lot. And he has a legitimate reason, because when Hiro was one month old, I went to work one day a week, and left the baby with him. There were a lot of reasons for taking that job. First of all, I had a serious cash-flow problem. I wasn't taking any courses until January, so my loans, my lovely loans, were coming due at twelve percent interest. Working one day a week just covered my monthly payments. At that time, I still split the home bills 50/50 with Brian; I used my government cheque, the Child Tax Benefit, for my share. (Child Tax Benefit is a beautiful thing. It means "groceries.") Our financial arrangements being what they were, I felt that I should be entitled to work as well as Brian, and furthermore, it didn't take a month to see that Hiro's care was going to be primarily my responsibility. I thought if Brian had Hiro for a day, especially on his own, without me to depend on or to interfere, it would be good for both of them.

And did I mention financial anxiety?

So when Shirley, my cousin and friend, asked me if I wanted to work one day a week filing in the office she managed, I said yes. They paid me respectably. I got out of the house.

The only problem was that Hiro literally screamed from the time I left until the time I came home at noon to feed him. If Brian was lucky, there would be a short afternoon nap after the feeding, and then Hiro would scream until I got home after work. I would walk through the door in the act of ripping off my blouse, seize the child and apply him to my engorged chest, while Brian collapsed on the bed in the fetal position. It was awful!

Brian often says he hates whiners. He whines as he says it, just to emphasize his point. Consequently, he will never tell me what's wrong. But he cannot escape his destiny. Having stopped up his mouth, he communicates with his whole body, every conceivable range of emotion. Wouldn't you say that the silent and immobile presence of a quaking lump, curled up like a hedgehog under the bedclothes, was a fairly clear message? Yet in his way Brian tried to be supportive of my needs. He wanted to be a good father and a good partner. He would not say "uncle."

Consequently, I kept on working, and how odd it felt to walk out the door free, no baby on my belly. Leaving Hiro was hard enough to make me feel deeply and truly grateful that I didn't have to work full time. Some women do, of course. Some women don't have access to that blessed invention, the maternity leave. Some women go right back to work after their babies are born. And while this is okay for some women, because the range of responses to something as shattering as motherhood is exceedingly vast, some women feel as I did, as though I was wearing my pajamas in public—cold, embarassed, vulnerable and *wrong*—but they have to go to work anyway.

And while we're on the topic, I'd like to spare a passing moment for women who have to give up their children for one reason or another. My whole body yearned for my baby, to the extent that thinking about him made my milk run down to my toes. Giving him up would have been an amputation. But some women have to do that, too.

I was glad I'd taken that first month off, to bask in the pleasure of my son! I didn't know I was going to get my job, but I did know I couldn't put my life on hold forever. I could see it coming: the grinding, the plodding. Life in a bachelor suite with a man who worked nights, a new baby, groceries to buy, housework to do, bills to pay, my essays to write, Brian's labs. (I hated those labs—I would rather write an essay myself than watch Brian write up a lab, trying to make some data he had collected at the university laboratory prove some stupid law of physics which was clearly meant to be a theoretical rather than a practical law. Ugg.)

And on top of this, my beloved Aunt Jean, for whom I had been doing part-time work all through university, had reached the stage where it was no longer safe for her to live alone. She wanted to finish her memoirs (which we had been writing together for about two years) before moving out to her daughter's place in the country. Suddenly, Christmas was our deadline. And it was a surprise to me—I'd counted on working on those memoirs for the rest of my life, I'd been doing it for so long.

I swear to God I don't know how I managed it all. I once heard what I believed to be an urban myth about a woman who did her bar exams and worked full time the year she had her second child. My sister-in-law (who told me this story) baby-sat this exceedingly over-competent woman's children (who were non-mythical, apparently well-adjusted, well-mannered, charming individuals). I nearly gagged on my jealousy. Not that I wanted her life; just that if she could do so much, why was I so overwhelmed with so little?

When my girlfriend told me she thought she'd like to combine going back to school for retraining with having a baby, I tried, as diplomatically as possible, to tell her, "Yes, yes, you *can* do that. If you have to, it *can* be done. You *can* do almost anything—you *will* do more than you ever thought possible—but you wouldn't want to, and you certainly shouldn't do it on purpose, as you value your sanity. If you have a choice, for heaven's sake, do your retraining before you get pregnant."

There is a theory floating among the mothers with whom I have compared notes that activity expands to fill the amount of time one has. For example, if one has a new baby, that consumes twenty-four hours a day. However, if one has three children, a full time job and a new puppy, that *also* consumes twenty-four hours a day. Taken to ridiculous lengths, according to this theory one can do all kinds of things, such as have another baby, take a lover, bake bread, or have a career, because the maximum amount of time the sum of all your activities can possibly take is twenty-four hours a day. I feel in my insecure soul that the horrible lawyer-woman who showed me up so badly must have magically put this principle into effect.

However, in actual fact, there is a kind of twenty-four-hours-in-a-day critical level, which can be likened to the rim of a big soup pot. Once the pot is full, it doesn't matter *what* you add—something else of equal mass is going to come out, because the pot only holds as much as it will hold. Nobody gets two pots, and twenty-four hours a day is all anyone gets.

If you are very fortunate, and very clever in the ways of the world, sometimes you will achieve a nice stew of a life, bubbling about two inches from the lip of the pot—a well-seasoned supper, a delicate blending of flavors, nourishing, sustaining, complete. But, if you're like me, you might get greedy, and try to put too much in the pot. A little of this, a little of that, and suddenly, there's no more room to simmer. The pot boils up all over the stove. Although, if I do say so myself, I make a damn fine stew.

Damn Fine Stew

Damn Fine Stew is made with anything you have in your fridge and cupboard, and is never the same twice. Follow these general directions, and away you go.

In a liberal amount of
olive oil in a Dutch oven, brown pieces of
chicken or **beef**—both is even better. This is a good meal for meat eaters who cannot bear to touch meat. Open the package of chicken, run water over it, and slide the chicken off the package into the hot oil. If you prefer beef, one small steak will do the trick. Cutting frozen steak in very thin slices does not count as touching meat—the squish factor just isn't there. Brown the meat with one or two
chopped onions and a couple of crushed
garlic cloves.

Vegetarians can start at this point, with the onions and garlic gently sizzling. Wash and chop more vegetables:
celery, carrots, green beans, corn, leeks, mushrooms.
Stay away from broccoli and cauliflower, as they tend to dominate the flavor of the stew. When everything has browned a bit, add
water or **stock.** Then you must add a
bay leaf, or even two, and some other herbs and spices:
thyme, marjoram, rosemary, and/or basil.

If you wish, add something hot:
cayenne, chili powder, sambal, or curry. Also
salt and **pepper.** At this point you can add
barley. Let the stew simmer a while before adding chunks of
potatoes, as potatoes get mushy easily, or
lentils, which cook very quickly.

When this mixture is almost cooked, you can begin to taste. If the stew is not flavorful enough, you can add
tomatoes, fresh, frozen, or by the can. You can also use
soy sauce, bouillon, a tablespoon of lemon juice or **fish sauce** if you like it. Especially if you're making a vegetarian stew, you might need, of all things, another tablespoon of
olive oil. I know it sounds strange, but sometimes it does the trick.

When the flavor is perfect, correct the texture. If the stew is too thick, add

water, stock or tomato juice. If it is too thin, take out about a half cup of liquid, cool it with an ice cube and then stir in either a couple of tablespoons of

flour or **cornstarch.** Either must be allowed to cook thoroughly before the stew can be eaten.

Now, if you like, make dumplings. Mix

1 cup flour (white, brown, cornmeal or a combination, but don't use all cornmeal or your dumplings will be very weird),

1 teaspoon baking powder

1/4 teaspoon salt

1 egg and

1/2 to 3/4 cup milk or water, depending on how much liquid the type of flour you've chosen soaks up. You don't want the batter runny. You must be able to spoon it. You may also use some dry herbs,

basil for example, if you want. Drop gently over the simmering stew, spoon by spoon, and let it cook fifteen minutes or so with the lid on the pot.

Damn fine stew.

SEVEN

When I think back on how we lived in that cramped space, struggling as we did, it seems so far away. I've been swimming through pea soup for so long now, it's hard to imagine the time when all this was new. But what choice did we have but to swim? One must either swim or drown. It's all very well to say that such and such will not matter in ten years, and indeed that may be true. But at the time, there is so much that needs to be done. Rent must be paid. Diapers must be washed. The essay which won't matter is a means to the degree which just might.

Nothing so very unusual has happened to me, in my insignificant little life. Who am I? Just a bug, just a grain of wheat. One of millions upon millions of mothers. But I remember thinking, "This is the childhood that is going to influence Hiroshi the rest of his life." So I refused to succumb to insignificance. The day-to-day drudgery that is such a huge part of motherhood—someone has to do it. I am part of the world. I am a part of the chain, and the chain is as strong as its weakest link. I am part of the web, and who is to say which span is important and which is not? Who sees the whole picture? Only the God, of whose existence I cannot be certain, much as I'd like to be, in a space and time where time and relevance do not exist: way far away from the immediate problem which is diaper rash or thrush or how to write an essay while nursing a baby.

And oh, how fast the time passes. And warps. And blurs. Hiroshi had a bad habit of waking up at 3:00 AM when his daddy came home from work (regularly, whether Brian worked or not). I used to strap him on and walk him up and down the street. I felt I'd rather risk the muggers than be evicted. (Joke, okay? It's a safe neighborhood.)

Lord, I was tired. Hazy to the level of blurred vision. And in addition to destroying my sleep patterns, Hiroshi decimated my focus and concentration. He was the king of continual interruptions. No wonder my sense of time and my grip on reality got mixed up! Disrupting concentration and sleep deprivation are both common brain-washing techniques. Call it "Initiation Ritual for the Parenting Club."

While I was losing mine, Hiroshi was developing a personality of his own. Instead of sleepers, he had little sweatshirts and overalls for the daytime. After Christmas he learned to sit propped up with pillows and play with his toys. I have a mental picture of him laughing, eyes shining, exhilarated by his new-found skill. The funny thing is, he looks now just like he did then, only older and less bald; but I couldn't see his future at the time. He had big brown eyes, flapping lashes, perfect skin and balanced features. He was built like I am, thin and wiry, so I hoped he'd get my physical strength too. Just like my father, he was never cold, and if you slept beside him, he gave off heat like a badly insulated oven. When he laughed from his belly, I ached with love.

And what reminded me of Brian? Hiro's sense of humor maybe. Brian had a whole array of good qualities I'd have been happy for Hiroshi to inherit, but the fact was, I couldn't see Brian in my son. The older he got, the more Hiro was like me. Sometimes I felt like he was cloned, not born. (*Is that who I would have been if I had been a boy?*) In some ways that was delightful, but in others, it was certainly less than flattering to see myself aped. And I hurt, knowing that so much of what caused me pain growing up was likely to cause him pain as well because he was so much like me.

I was walking around with Hiroshi one day and this old guy out for his constitutional stopped me, pointed at Hiro and said, "He's going to be forty in about ten minutes." That being so, there wasn't much point in worrying about what was going to happen in the interim, was there? Or maybe there was, because just as Hiroshi was learning to sit up (little boy-man in his striped T-shirt, very macho, very cool), President Bush sent his country to war with Iraq.

The miserable state of the world had always been my number-one reason for not wanting children. This is no place for tender creatures, I thought. (As for tough creatures, we have enough of those.) The Gulf War was my first major disaster after Hiro came into our lives, and while I hadn't really expected the-powers-that-be to conduct themselves peacefully just because I'd had a baby, I took it hard.

There I was, absolutely preoccupied with life force while the media obsessed on death force. I wept for the children, I prayed for the mothers of the soldiers, and above all, I prayed for the Earth, that poor abused body upon which we depend totally. Oh, I know that it's not so straightforward, the politics of war and peace. However, it seemed to me that the bottom line was clear: if we destroyed the Earth, all our fights, large and small, would suddenly cease to matter. Disagreement would be a luxury we would no longer be able to demand, because without the Earth, we'd be dead.

One newscast a day was all I could handle. Brian, on the other hand, followed the Gulf Crisis like the Superbowl. He glued himself to the radio. My mother, who was visiting, bought him a converter so he could use the headphones, and I wouldn't have to hear history in the making from second to second. And there he sat, hallucinating, I assume, experiencing virtual reality (rigid and twitching in the armchair) taking in the news intravenously, mumbling, "Mayday, mayday." He was no help at all in terms of maintaining perspective.

Yet ultimately, the Gulf War barely touched me. I cared more than ever that we were ruining our planet, since I desperately wanted a place for Hiro to stand and air for him to breathe, but there seemed little I could do. The force of my passion, the power of my desire wasn't going to soothe the world into placidity.

In a way I was ashamed to let go of my fear and rage, as if emotional turmoil was some kind of super-glue holding the world together, and if I stopped paying attention, the forces of gravity would suddenly cease to function and we'd all be reduced to ions and float free into space. And it would be all my fault, because of my unnatural apathy. However, in the end I simply had to stop freaking out. It wasn't helping anything, least of all Hiroshi.

My deadlines were closing in, so apocalyptic oil fields burned while I busied myself more than ever. I had finished Aunt Jean's memoirs by Christmas, which was satisfying, but I still had a couple of essays to write, and I started my last required course in January. My newly found discipline amazed me. I worked like a donkey to finish that degree. Going to work at the office once a week was by comparison relaxing. I was so busy, I wanted to have my picture taken as I sat cross-legged on the toilet, peeing and nursing Hiroshi while I brushed my teeth with my spare hand, but the camera was that one detail just over my maximum limit of capability.

Mind you, Hiroshi didn't suffer. I need to assure you of this. Women these days have this huge guilt thing: am I spending enough time, enough *quality* time, with my child? We must give give give, till our guts come out our noses, but at the same time, there is a pressure to succeed succeed succeed. "You can have it all!" sings a merry tune, but listen to the harmony: "You *should* have it all, or you're not doing it right."

And this obsessive concern with our children's little psyches, this neurotic fear of somehow inadvertently inflicting psychological damage, this is new, according to my aunt. She said she cheerfully raised her five children, doing what had to be done, until her second was a teenager, and then suddenly there was a big increase in women's magazines, all of which seemed to say that no matter how your child turned out, it was the mother's fault. She said she switched to fiction at that time, having decided that the magazines printed lies and fairy tales, and she'd rather take her stories straight up than parading as the truth.

I know my mother certainly didn't spend a lot of time with us, aside from performing the nightly bedtime story marathon. Good gracious, she had a husband, a hired man, a huge garden, all our clothes to make, and, during harvest, a truck to drive as well. She didn't have a lot of leisure after essentials were taken care of. (But I do remember she was there when I most needed her to talk to or to hold.) Later, she stopped driving the truck but she taught kindergarten part time. Still, the job was for her satisfaction, to keep her sane and whole; she was not expected to work outside the home. My father accepted rather than demanded my mother's employment.

But in my generation women are doubly damned. We feel guilty when we leave our children to go to work, and we feel guilty when we stay home and don't bring in an income. My defensive reaction, as I wrestled to finish my degree and care for my son, turned out to be only the beginning of my conflicting emotions over Hiroshi's needs and financial necessity.

When Hiroshi was awake, I couldn't do schoolwork. He rapidly got used to getting all the attention he wanted because I felt I couldn't let him cry. First of all there was the apartment thing—this was prior to legislation preventing discrimination against children in rental units and our rent was relatively low; I didn't want my neighbors complaining and I didn't want to move. Secondly, Brian had to sleep. He was still working nights, taking courses and watching Hiro on my office day (which rapidly became known as "Jo's Tuesday off"). Hiro was still at an age when I could just put him under one arm, so to speak, and do whatever I had to do, so I took him out a lot. He was restaurant trained (yippee!) and when the regular office secretary called in sick, I brought Hiroshi to the office and answered phones. It was a very low-key office at that time. That's the beauty of one child. One child, two hands, you're still ahead of the game.

I couldn't take him to class though. I couldn't keep him quiet enough, and I didn't think that was fair to the other kids—and I mean kids. I was a mature student to begin with, and since I'd had Hiroshi I felt like a tourist traveling in a foreign land. Every now and then I'd have a relapse: Friday afternoon would roll around and I'd think, "Why aren't I in the pub?" But by 6:00, by the time we were finished suppers and baths, the feeling would be long gone and I'd yearn for bedtime. All those twenty-year-olds up at the university, schmoozing around each other like dogs in heat; I wanted to scream at them, "Wrap that rascal! One baby will mess up your whole social life!"

See, it's no wonder I continued to smoke. It felt like the only thing that was left to me which was mine alone. Couldn't drink, couldn't party, nothing but baby and work work work. I tried over and over again to quit, but nicotine is my drug. Plus I couldn't smoke around Hiroshi. I didn't want to damage his lungs, regardless of what I was willing to do to my own. Hence, I had a foolproof excuse for taking a short break from his constant demands, stepping outside, and closing the door. We lived on the ground floor. Our entrance opened onto the parking lot, so I could peer in our window and wave. There are a lot of mothers out there, surreptitiously smoking on balconies.

When I did quit smoking, whether it was for one day or three weeks, I noticed that I never got a break. I never stopped working, except to play with Hiroshi. I never sat down except to give my son attention. As a non-smoker, I might plan to take a coffee break just for me, but I never got around to it.

But I had to smoke, or my body screamed at me. And so I had to take a break.

I got my friend Sarah, who is half a decade younger than I am, to baby-sit for me while I did my classes twice a week. This was a very good thing for her. She had a strong desire to have a child, but as I always say, there's nothing like baby-sitting to improve birth control.

"Listen," I told her. "Falling in love is a false cathartic experience triggered by your biological clock, and the hormone that kept our ancestors from dropping all their useless baby bundles on the trail to be eaten by the wolves will keep you from throwing your baby under a bus. You will be tricked by nature all round. How humiliating!" I also informed her that she had been misled by the media, whose images of love and devotion bore no relation at all to *my* reality, and to prove it, I re-worded some of my sappy old pop songs, my personal favorite being, "I've been peed on, I've been puked on, when will I be loved?" which I'm sure Linda Ronstadt could sing with great elegance.

My real ace for Sarah, though, was the spiel on gross things that happen to your body. I told her about vaginal mucus and hemorrhoids, varicose veins and stretch marks, and how you drip from every orifice during pregnancy. I told her about the exercise you must do every day for the rest of your life when you're waiting in checkout lines if you want to have total control over when you pee and when you don't, especially when you sneeze or run.

I told her about heartburn and how the baby takes so much space that your diaphragm gets pushed and your whole digestive system revolts and you get constipated. I told her how your bones get loose and you have to sleep with every part of you propped up on either side, or the weight of those parts hanging down will painfully stretch the skin that is supporting them. I told her how your breasts get huge, monumental, and they're under pressure like a full bladder, so that if you wait too long to feed your baby, they will leak and if you squeeze them, they will shoot milk clear across the room. I told her how, once you've weaned your baby, every part of you that was once full will hang like a beanbag, and I sang for her:

> *Do your tits hang low?*
> *Do they waggle to and fro?*
> *Can you tie 'em in a knot?*
> *Can you tie 'em in a bow?*
> *Can you sling 'em over your shoulder*
> *Like a continental soldier?*
> *Do your tits hang low?*

"Sarah," I said seriously, "this is not a romantic experience." And she would watch me dandle my son while I gave her this most edifying lecture, and listen to me not one whit!

Did you notice I haven't been talking about food for a while? Actually, I did make lunch for Sarah so she could eat before babysitting, and she was a culinary challenge because of a long string of life-threatening allergies, in addition to her personal commitment not to eat meat. It was because of her that I learned to make split-pea soup flavored with garlic and thyme instead of ham bone, and black bean soup with olives and cumin. What I was really in search of, however, was a cookbook entitled *Quick Cooking for People Who Have To Do It*, or *The Fast, the Easy and the Cheap, for People Who Have to Eat*. I was looking for a book with a series of delicious rotating menus, guaranteeing a balanced diet, complete with weekly grocery lists and what to do with leftovers, so I would not have to think at all. Of course, even if I could find such a book, it would never work for me because I cannot bear green peppers or cabbage. They are simply too hard for me to digest.

However, I did begin to collect recipes that worked in a series. For example, Sarah gave me a recipe for chickpeas with garlic and onions, dressed with olive oil, lemon, basil, salt and pepper. These are great in a pita with fresh lettuce and tomatoes and yogurt (the tomatoes had to be fried for Sarah, because raw tomatoes would make her keel over dead). This is truly delicious and very filling.

Then some of the leftover chickpeas go into a chicken soup stock with some couscous, tofu, baby corn and fish sauce. (Brian won't eat fish sauce. By the time you're third-generation Canadian, you've earned the right to hate fish and anything even remotely resembling fish if you want to, even if your Japanese ancestors shudder in their graves. But so much for the soup; I made only what Hiro and I could eat for lunch.)

The rest of the chickpeas went into a pasta salad, onions and all, along with olives, cheeses and vegetables in oregano red-wine vinegar dressing. That's a complete meal, right there, and it's beautiful too if you use tri-color pasta, and Brian would scarf it right down because whatever caused him to loathe fish did not in the least affect his Oriental passion for noodles in any shape or form.

There! Three meals disposed of: cheap, good, nutritious, fast. That was my focus, and why not? I loved university; I loved it very much, but that last year, I just wanted to get that damn degree done. All my endurance was bent in this direction: to do what I had to do and be done with it, as efficiently as possible. And I cooked the same way.

Emergency Supper

(My Mother Used To Do This, So It Must Be Okay, Right?)

Emergency supper is pancakes. They're fast, they're easy, and unless you're allergic to eggs, all the ingredients are in the house. Children usually love them, and if you make pancakes with whole-wheat flour, they're a sinless treat.

The key to good pancakes is to make them often. That way, it is possible to remember exactly which setting on the stove creates perfectly cooked pancakes, neither burned nor underdone. Also, you remember how thin to make the batter. These details vary from family to family and the more often you make pancakes, the less of a production they are.

Here are the dry ingredients:
1 cup whole-wheat flour
1 teaspoon baking powder
1 tablespoon sugar
1/4 teaspoon salt

Do we measure? No way! Pancakes are very forgiving, and like I said, the oftener you make 'em, the faster you get.

While you're mixing that, preheat your skillet. Cast iron is good, medium heat works best. The object is to find the perfect heat, so that you can turn the stove on and never touch that dial.

Now add the wet ingredients:
1 egg
1 tablespoon vegetable oil
milk, or water if you have an allergy.

Use enough liquid to make the batter the right thickness. We like our pancakes thin, but suit yourself. If you use a thicker batter, use a lower heat too, or your pancakes will be raw in the middle.

Mix the batter, put some oil in the skillet and dump in your first load. Flip when your pancake is making bubbles. You're on your way. Don't forget: the object is not to have a nice, relaxed, sit-down meal, but rather to feed those kids and get them out of your hair.

Two tips for beginners: If you have two children, don't make one big pancake. Make two little ones. That way you will avoid the fight over who gets the first pancake. Second, if you haven't already introduced your children to syrup, don't. Give them fruit sauce on their pancakes, or even jam. But once they know about syrup, there's no going back. That's what they'll want—of course. It's sugar. "My First Drug." *Zing.*

EIGHT

All my passions had taken a very practical turn. Hiroshi was my passion. Hiroshi was my miracle, my magic, he was all that was mysterious and good. But his survival was a practical matter, no doubt about that. This blending of the ephemeral and the never-ending, of the astonishing and the mundane, affected every aspect of my life, including my relationship with Brian.

Remember him? The father of my child? This is how things were going with my Mr. Brian: I dreamed I was with my ex-husband. (Yes, I have one—I married young and stupid, and got the divorce experience out of the way early.) This was very irritating to me. My ex was hard enough to ditch the first time. But in my dream, I finally accomplished my freedom, and I looked across an open field and saw my new lover, dressed in a long black cloak, floating toward me, and then up into the air. Awareness hit me like a nice refreshing glass of chilled vinegar. "Oh my God," I thought, "I'm going out with Dracula!"

Frankly, all was not clear between Brian and me. When I got pregnant, I got a whole new life almost instantly. Everything, but everything, bent toward Hiroshi. Yes, I still had courses and my friends and my little jobs, but as far as I was concerned, the solar system had a new sun.

Brian, on the other hand, still had his old life. He had a degree to complete, a living to earn, and all his old friends to play with. The baby was simply one more thing. Oh yes, Hiro was wonderful, but having an infant was really hard for Brian. Hiro pooped, and screamed. Brian was fastidious and sensitive to loud noises.

I had the breasts, I had the opinions, I was the one with all the passion. I felt like I was dragging Brian along.

And how did that happen? I had mixed feelings about where I stood within a cultural framework. It could have been argued that I was a very good woman for having extended Brian's line by presenting him with a son and heir. Doesn't every man, from the greatest monarch to the lowest peon, want a son and heir?

But we have other cultural stereotypes, just as strong perhaps, for surprise pregnancies. We have the Venus-flytrap woman, that conniving she-witch who uses her sexual powers to seduce the unsuspecting male who does not recognize the womb as a weapon which will trap him into doing "the honorable thing" and tie him to domesticity and tedium forever. We also have the lecherous male who gets the gullible girl knocked up and must be pressured into a shotgun wedding. And both scenarios focus on taking freedom away from the male. Whether a man be Fool or Libertine, whether a woman be Victim or Siren, no acknowledgment is given to the freedom the female might be losing; no mention is made of what the baby might be feeling.

In spite of my mental rejection of these images, the crux of my personal problem lay in the fact that I had intuitive knowledge from the moment of conception that I was going to have a baby. I knew, and I didn't give Brian a fair choice.

I don't know whether Brian agreed with me or not (it was never discussed), but I felt I owed him one, for taking away his decision-making power. For not giving him a fair chance on a level playing field to choose whether we would have a child or not. After I got pregnant, he got no choice at all, other than to stay or leave, and I knew well enough Brian could not abandon us, given his moral persuasion. The rapid exit was not an option for him. Yes, he loved me, but love had nothing to do with it. According to Brian, honorable men did not desert women who got pregnant. It simply Wasn't Done.

Mind you, when I picked up the tab at the banquet of guilt, my female friends didn't just sit there sympathizing and sipping their coffee, doing the share-and-tell routine we all learn as infant baby girls ("I know what you mean, you wouldn't believe what happened to my Aunt Mathilda"). When I told women that I felt I needed to put more into running the household because I'd sort of coerced Brian into having a baby, they tended to spew flak. They went off like machine guns, rat-a-tat-tat. They didn't want to hear it, and I knew why.

My friends exploded because women are damned tired and resentful of being assigned the blame and responsibility for pregnancy and for taking freedom away from men. It takes two to make a baby, guys. If you don't like surprises, take action! Roll on that rubber, or keep your pecker in your paw. Women find it hard to be neutral on this issue. Especially since it keeps happening. A woman thinks she's in an equal, caring, sharing relationship, and suddenly—whoops! There's this cultural banana peel and zoom, she's flat on her back with Mr. Sensitive New Age Guy standing over her expostulating, "Where is the life that late I led?"

Yep, it happened to me. You know what it was like? It was like when you really want to go to see a play, but your partner isn't so keen on it. But you *really* want to go, so you drag your partner off to this play, and it's just awful. The acting sucks, the lighting is bad, and the script just doesn't have it. It's the worst play you've ever had to sit through. It's the worst play you've ever paid good money to see. And guess what. It was *your* idea. Maybe your partner is sweet enough not to rub it in, but it was still your idea.

Well, much as Brian loved his son, whenever anything went wrong, mmmm, what's that ugly smell, wafting through the room like burnt toast—oh, yeah, *eau de* "Your Idea."

And while we're laboring with rage, women resent the subtle change that comes with age and children, from attractive, sexual female to bovine breeder, a possession and responsibility, either an albatross around some guy's neck or a burden on society. (Oh, children are so valuable in our culture!) And whether your partner espouses these stereotypes or not, we are all affected by this picture, the same way we are all affected by the fact that collectively, we value thinness and youth. You can fight it with liposuction, or you can look at yourself in the mirror every morning and say, "You are beautiful, just the way you are." The very fact that you need to do those things means that you are still affected by cultural values.

But I felt guilty, all theory not withstanding, and consequently, what happened was that our whole domestic environment (and it did not help that Brian had moved into my apartment, not I into his) became my domain. I did it all—if Brian wanted to stay, that was his business. The shopping, the housework, the laundry, the cooking, anything to do with child-rearing—those were my responsibilities. I wanted it perfectly clear that as far as I was concerned, Brian could leave if he wanted to. Sometime in the new year, we negotiated a change of our finances. Brian paid more bills in acknowledgment that I was spending more time on maintaining our home. We slid into traditional roles like a knife into a sheath.

I ate a lot of resentment because my bottom line was that I wanted Hiroshi to have a father. I had a father. Fathers are great! Lots of kids don't have a father. Lots of kids are better off without one. But Hiroshi had a father. Hiroshi had a good father. I thought I'd keep him.

But you see, what I just said (and how I said it), illustrates the other side of the double standard. Maybe over the years, patriarchy and the church have tried to take the power away from us, but what I feel in my gut (and I know a lot of women feel this way) is that Woman Rules. Woman knows her body and her baby. Woman is the core; all the other stuff may be important, but it's peripheral to the core. No wonder men had to put us down, burn us at the stake as witches. We are too powerful, in a way patriarchy as a system is hard pressed to control—powerful with life. Yes, I have felt less-than, under-than, imposed-upon at times in my life. That was all exterior. On the inside, power! Life! And during that particular present, fierce maternal energy, to do what had to be done and get what I needed for my baby!

So actually, I was quite prepared to take on the grunt work, and while I did so, I belittled Brian's part.

"Yeah, it would be nice if you'd stay and be a part of our family, but we don't really need you, you're a perk, not a necessity."

Or "I want Hiroshi to have a father and a good education. Hmm, let's see—I'll keep the dad, and go buy the education." See what I mean?

No doubt Brian had an entirely different point of view.

Jo's Finest Chicken Stuffing

(For Incredibly Self-Righteous Stuffed-Shirts Like Me
or for People with a Lot of Gender *Stuff*
or Whoever Else is Hungry)

Actually, the recipe for this chapter should have been something that
you ignite *Poof, Wow!* and it bursts into flames. But I don't know how
to make anything like that, and while I have a fair bit of experience as
pyro-cook, I've never come up with anything burned that I'd be pleased
to repeat. So I decided to settle for stuffing, which is delicious.

Take your chicken (or turkey) and wash it out. If you like, you can
rub the inside with a
garlic clove, but I will understand if you choose not to. There's a
limit to how much contact one wants with a cold, wet fowl.

In a generous bowl, mix:
1 cup cubed bread pieces
1 cup slow-cooking rolled oats
1/2 cup pine nuts and/or sunflower seeds
a minced onion
**1 teaspoon poultry seasoning or 1/2 teaspoon each rosemary,
thyme, and sage**
1 teaspoon salt
garlic powder, if desired.

Now, you must decide how moist you like your stuffing. For these
proportions (which I have never measured in my life until I tried to
write down the recipe), I use about
3/4 cup water, but I'm afraid you must experiment to get this recipe
perfect for your personal taste.

And that's all there is to it. Stuff that bird and pop it in the oven. Put
it on the table and swoon with joy.

NINE

In spite of my excuse that smoking was the only recreation left to me which was mine and mine alone (my rest, my break, my treat, my bribe), it was no accident that I started smoking shortly after my father died. "What! Life is not going to last forever!? You mean I too will someday die, and furthermore no one knows the day or the hour?! Then truly, why shouldn't I flirt with Death—Death is flirting with me!"

When I smoked, I always tipped my hat to Death. "Hello," sez I. "Nice night for it."

"Evenin'," sez Death, "Jist passin' through."

We both pulled our long gray mackintoshes more tightly up to our ears, mashed our Bogart hats a little lower and moseyed down dirty, twilight streets, cigarette butts clenched tightly between thumb and finger, slow smoke curling behind us as we scuffed the sidewalk. Romantic, no? Trouble, stress of any kind makes me want to smoke: anything, from war, to ecological apocalypse, to famine, to domestic dispute, but above all else, fear of economic failure makes me weak-kneed with desire to light up.

Which is why I mention it. The closer I got to the end of my university degree, the more pressure I felt to decide what I was going to do with myself, specifically, to support myself. More specifically, to ensure Hiroshi's and my own financial security and happiness forever. Unfortunately, I wasn't any closer to knowing what I wanted to do than I had been in high school.

Actually, I've always had plenty of things to do—it's things to do that will make money that I have a problem with. I really believe that if I had ever, in the past twenty years, made it an exclusive priority to have lots and lots of money, I would have. But I never did.

My parents can take some of the blame. They were thoughtful people who discussed things with their children. Politics, sex, religion, and why we had a Datsun instead of a big, gas-guzzling American car. My parents were the original advocates of the simple life, limiting our extra activities to save time for dreaming and reading, encouraging us to put our faith in our selves, not our things. Never once did I hear "Thou shalt earn a lot of dough." It was "Stand up, put your shoulders back, think for yourself. Treat this planet and everything on it, including you, with respect."

And then, as if my parents hadn't been weird enough, my high school social studies teacher put the final nail in my financial coffin. How I admired him. He taught us about the Third World, and that a small percentage of the world's population was consuming a huge percentage of the world's resources. It was my first exposure to eco-apocalypse (other than Mother making me wash out my plastic baggies all those years, that is).

So, while I had no alternative plan to speak of, I consciously decided to reject what looked to me like a straight path from the cradle to the grave, amassing wealth, consuming resources, procreating and leaving a trail of garbage behind me. Instead of going straight to technical school to pick out a dining card, I headed off to Mexico to live with a Spanish family (they were very conservative, by the way, which is amusing in retrospect, since I was trying so hard not to be). Thus began my career on the fringe, and highly diverting it has been, too!

But although I never set out to be "established," the deal was that I would always support myself. I never wanted to be a burden on society. Or add another little baby burden. I was supposed to put in, not drain out. That was my image of myself.

And remember that I said every parent gets at least one Big Surprise in the child-rearing department? And I was the one who thought she would just pop baby into daycare and head off to work? Guess what. My number came up. I had no idea, no inkling under the sun, how strongly I would feel that I didn't want Hiroshi in daycare. The very thought made me feel physically ill, and the fact that Brian completely agreed with me has made every day of my life as a mother easier. At least I haven't had to push against my partner's subtle pressure.

Furthermore, I had no idea how incredibly expensive daycare is. Either you have to make so much money that you can afford daycare or a nanny, or else you must make so little that the government prefers to subsidize your daycare rather than support you on welfare. What that boiled down to for me was that there was no point in putting Hiroshi in daycare and going off to be a secretary like I was before. Because of my student loans, I could not pay someone to look after my child, support myself, and stay solvent on minimum wage or anything near it. If I was going to work full time, I had to make more money. I had to get myself a Real Career.

I told myself, "Okay, girl. Keep up, Jo Jones. It's time to join the middle class."

My parents started out small. They set up housekeeping in a tiny space with second-hand furniture and hand-me-down baby clothes. They worked hard and prospered and got older and told stories about how they used to go to bed at night and feel the holes in the sheets with their toes. There may not have been much, but as a child I never went hungry, not a day in my life. I grew up in complete security—so why am I so afraid of the world? Were the horrors that drove my starving, potato-fed ancestors out of Europe (and Brian's millet-fed ancestors from Japan) so great that the shock waves reverberate down to my generation? *War* (whack), *Pestilence* (whack), *Famine* (whack), like being hit on the back by a long two-by-four. Or maybe what I hear on the news is real enough, terrifying enough to keep fear dogging my heels forever.

Enough. As I said, I grew up in security, and I felt it incumbent upon me to provide the same for my son. While there was nothing I could do about war, pestilence and famine, surely money would provide a degree of safety. It wasn't that I wanted Nikes and a minivan, matching dishware and summers at hockey camp for Hiroshi. I just wanted to pay my bills and survive. I wanted a cushion in case of emergency. I wanted regular money coming in. Real money. More than enough. Clearly I needed what nearly everyone has always strongly suggested I acquire: a profession. Better late than never, right? Deep sigh.

While I was going through university, like every other serious English major I thought about going on in English, getting the Master's degree and becoming a professor. That was my excuse for taking that luscious undergrad degree. I suppose it might have worked if I hadn't had Hiroshi, but I did. And after I had Hiroshi, Hiroshi was what I was interested in. The supposed profession was for his sake, not mine. Academia is competitive enough that I knew I couldn't succeed without passion to drive me. And besides, I knew three English professors personally who never read for pleasure. Can you imagine? The paucity of their lives. It would be like working in a coffee shop and learning to associate the smell of the brew with work.

So doing a Master's was out. Or indefinitely on hold. I narrowed my options down to teaching and dental hygiene. I thought I could get some grace time from my student loans (I was wrong) and start taking courses so that by the time I was ready to let go of Hiroshi a little, I'd be employable. In the meantime—teaching/dental hygiene, dental hygiene/teaching. Both my grandmothers, all my aunts and my mother were teachers. I felt sure I could do primary grades, though teenagers would have me for breakfast, no doubt. I needed a university science course to get into the program, but once I had that, I could be a teacher in two short years. My English degree took three years off the regular course work; at least it was good for that much. And teachers only work from September to June. I could be off work when Hiroshi was out of school.

Too bad I felt wretched just thinking about it.

As for becoming a dental hygienist, the appeal was that for some odd reason, they were in demand on the job market. They made $27 an hour. For that kind of coin, I figured eventually I could work part time and support myself very nicely by sticking my fingers into other people's mouths. But I needed biology, chemistry and psychology to get into the program. And there was a waiting list of dental wannabes.

Teaching/dental hygiene, dental hygiene/teaching—remember when we were growing up and our guidance counselors told us to choose work we thought we'd like to do? Remember the expectation that we would find meaningful work? Of course we were in our primo egocentric phase then; did even one of us turn around and ask our counselor if he/she liked what she/he did? Probably not.

This career stuff—I obviously didn't get it. I just didn't understand the emphasis some people placed on their work. In the spring, I went to the divisional meeting for the company I filed for on Tuesdays. Lots and lots of boring speeches. Of course, all those bigwigs had careers, whereas I had a job, which as a matter of principle I wanted to do my best at. But as I sat and listened to the company brass talk abut Team Spirit, Motivational Marketing and Unified Vision, how trivial it all seemed in comparison to the simple acts involved in caring for my boy. The job is a means to feed the baby, okay? That's all it is. Doing a good job is a moral issue, but the point is to feed that baby. But then again, the top dogs were all shareholders, so they stood to gain personally from our individual motivation. So perhaps we were not so differently motivated after all, they and I.

I decided to put off making a decision. Brian had another year of university to do and he was essentially supporting us all by working in the bar. After I graduated (a completely unmarked passage) I got myself enrolled in the summer psychology course. I registered to take a couple of science courses in the fall semester. I prepared my mind to be in university a little longer and to be in debt a lot longer. I tried not to wonder when and if I'd get to have another baby.

Another baby!

Brian was beside himself. I didn't have the first one sleeping through the night, let alone the means to secure his future, and I wanted to double my trouble. To Brian, it simply didn't make sense. But my desire for a second child was beyond financial or logical reasoning. One is an accident, you cope with it. Or if you're a yuppie, one is an acquisition: got the house (check), got the car (check), got the kid (check). But two is a family. One is lonely, all alone during times of crisis, but whether you like your siblings or not, family is family when the chips are down.

Both Brian and I come from strong families. In fact, one of the undeserved perks I got when I brainlessly chose Brian for his sex appeal was that he came with the best set of parents a daughter-in-law could ever wish for. Not only were they good to me, but, after all those years of marriage, they were still good to each other, which boded well to those of us who believe that people tend to repeat their parents' patterns.

Goodness knows it's easier to pass on a tradition of family which goes back for generations than to try to create one out of the blue, from scratch, with no successful models closer to the heart than the happy families on TV. Brian and I knew what kind of home life we were trying to make for Hiroshi, but to me, an only child didn't complete the picture. Something was glaringly missing.

However, I couldn't see how I was going to get my own way, go to school and pay the bills. My intuition, my sense of "rightness" saw a second child—my logic, my sense of "how it is" didn't. Trying to reconcile my intuition with my logic cost me a lot of mental energy and worry. (I should have known better! Head is good, but heart rules. Forever and ever.)

Anyway, I felt better knowing I had a plan for the time being. I like to have a plan. I want to be in control. I want security (against pain, want, hardship) and I keep on fighting, fighting for it, even though I believe we were put on this Earth to learn to live without it. Why can't I just give up, and consider the flowers of the field? Do the best that I can, and trust in the future? Believe there is a reason, and live with honor? In the end, when we grow up, when we *really* grow up, we are all equal and the same on this Earth: six feet under, pushing up daisies. I know the answer to that one. I'm afraid that if I make the wrong choices, I'll end up living like a troll under a bridge in some dirty downtown core. I'm afraid I'll slip through the cracks, into the ever-widening gap between rich and poor, till I can't afford even the things I consider absolute essentials, like calcium, or antibiotics when we're sick. I'm afraid I'll get stuck doing something totally hateful to me day after day, till my bones turn to powder and, like the Musicians of Bremen, no one wants me any more. Then I tell myself, "If the worst comes to the worst, and life becomes unbearable, you can always kill yourself. Sure. You've had a good life, a damn fine life, you don't have to live miserably until you die."

(But what about my baby! How that baby does complicate things!)

Leek and Potato Soup

(A Recipe Against the Cold)

To me there is nothing more efficacious for squelching the fear of living under a bridge than a steaming bowl of soup with bread and cheese. I'm not sure why this should be so. You'd think a big fat steak or lobster would be more connotative of wealth and security. Feeling poor? Pass the sirloin. If you're eating beef, there can't be much of a problem.

But no. When I'm feeling afraid of my future, the best possible thing to do is make a pot of soup. I think the comfort lies in thinking, "Well, look, here I am eating this wonderful meal for just pennies a bowl. Give me a pot and a hot plate and that's all I need to whip it up. No matter how bad it gets, I'll survive, because I'm a survivor. Mmmm. Good soup!"

Take a sturdy pot and sauté
one leek, chopped very fine in
oil or butter. Don't have a leek? Use
onion, or both. When the leek is tender, add
2 or 3 potatoes diced small. Put enough water to barely cover the vegetables and cook until tender. Then add
3 cups of milk and heat but do not boil. Season with
salt, pepper and cayenne.

Like almost all of my favorite recipes, this one is flexible.
Celery and
sliced mushrooms make nice additions; so do
carrot slivers and
corn.
Thyme, paprika, garlic, or
a pinch of sugar can all be used to vary the flavor.
Sliced green onions sprinkled on top of the soup make it look more elegant than it is.

Check your fridge and suit yourself. This is something from nothing. Gotta like that.

TEN

And so I entered the fast-food phase of my life. My brief but truly intense attempt to join the rat race. I didn't even make it through the preliminary heat.

But first, I had an absolutely fabulous summer. The prof who taught my psych course was a realist. She did not even expect us to come to class and told us if we were capable of passing exams by reading the text, we were welcome to work that way. Which I did, sitting in the park with Hiroshi, going through the flash cards I'd prepared the night before. Hiro was happy, as long as I was there. He didn't need anyone to play with and he entertained himself. Hanging out at the neighborhood spot of green—huge umbrella leaves protecting us, Hiroshi pushing the stroller. That's what he did, all summer long.

Under the main frame, the stroller had a strong bar which supported Hiroshi's weight (because he wasn't actually walking yet) while he supplied the forward force. If I put one back brake on, the stroller went round and round and round in a big circle, and for a long time Hiro was satisfied with that. When he discovered the brake release, I had to work a little harder, chasing him across the park and back.

Or we'd play in the graveyard on the way to the store. Blue sky, blue ocean in the distance, manicured grass, big trees, Hiroshi's little bare bum (fresh air does wonders for diaper rash), chubby little legs, dimpled hands reaching to catch the bubbles I blew for him—all God's blessings—and Private Norman Medley's gravestone, dead at the tender age of twenty in 1918, probably of influenza. This, to make my minutes more precious, to remind me of an end to excess, a taste of bitter, to make the cloying sweetness more delicious. In short, the very kind of thing I love the most.

Then we'd go home and make supper and that was always awful, because no matter how lovely and sweet-tempered your child is, no one escapes Hell Hour, which is the hour just before supper, usually between four and five. Is it that they're hungry then? You know, I really don't think so, because I didn't much care if Hiroshi ate when we did; I fed him when he wanted to eat. (This method developed because I eat all the time. I never go anywhere without snacks. It seemed a little silly to tell him he couldn't eat between meals when I constantly did.) I also thought perhaps the witching hour occurred because mothers get cooking, and children sense that they no longer have one hundred percent attention. But no. Even if we were having something extremely low maintenance, like pre-made throw 'er-in-the-oven casserole (lasagna, or maybe chopped pork sausages, sautéed onions and garlic, black olives and brown rice in a savory tomato sauce—make four, freeze three), Hiroshi was (*is*) horrible between four and five.

He would crawl around the kitchen, strategically placing himself where I next wanted to step, whining and whimpering, till I thought I would lose my mind and punt him through the doorway. And my mother's echo would be there, her stories about how she would stir the gravy with one hand (Daddy was definitely a meat and potatoes kind of guy) and hold me to her hip with the other, because I was the ultimate Hell Hour Horror Child. Then I would reach down and pull Hiroshi to me and love him all up the way I would have wanted to be loved if I was still the whiner on the floor. (That, by the way, was on a good day. On a bad day I'd scream, "Brian! Get this kid away from me, I'm losing it!" And very glad I was to have that option to exercise, too. How *do* single mothers cope?!)

I used to think people wanted grandchildren for the sake of having grandchildren, but now I realize revenge is a big motivator. I found myself thinking, "Dear Hiro, you too will have children, and serve you right." My mother used to say that to me. I heard her voice coming out of my mouth more and more. One big benefit of having children is that you begin to identify with your parents, which is mind stretching. I discussed this phenomenon with Mom and she told me she was having a similar psychological "bonding experience" with her grandmothers. This is the beauty of generations—you can feel the wheel, where you fit in it, and how it is going round and round. Of course, for some people the paramount part of that experience is consciously breaking the circle, but for other, more fortunate individuals, round is a beautiful feeling.

This being the case, you are probably going to think I'm a real idiot when I tell you I was well into my first year with Hiroshi when it occurred to me, "Hey! My mother loved me as much as I love my boy. This is what she meant when she said she loved me. Oh my God, she loved me this much!" I always thought she meant she loved me the way I loved her, which I did, and do, very much—but not the way I love Hiroshi! Sure, Mom tried to explain it to me often enough, but I only *really* believed in a love as great as that which I myself felt. I was so shocked I had to sit down. To be loved so, and not to know it!

And how much farther does this stretching go? All my life I've heard that "God is love," and basically thought, "Yeah, and boxed breakfast cereal with five ounces of milk is a good source of protein." However, my love for Hiroshi was so much greater than anything I'd ever experienced before that the possibility that unconditional and infinite love might actually exist, far beyond the comprehension of my puny mind, seemed almost plausible for the first time. If Hiroshi, then God. Logic!

★★★★★

My golden summer! Ah yes! Then, about the last week in August, the shine picked up its boots and left. We moved upstairs in the same apartment building, into a one-bedroom suite. And of course that was awful; moving always is and Brian especially hates it because he has all the flexibility and speed of a glacier when it comes to change. I told my friends I wished we'd gone somewhere that had an elevator, because I never wanted to move with Brian again and I was going to have a lot of trouble with his wheelchair on those stairs when he was ninety and I eighty-six. But there was a lot of space, comparatively, and oh, we were sophisticated! My, my! And there was a real kitchen, not a galley, so we actually gained two rooms.

Then university started for Brian and me, and that was a feat in juggling. First thing in the morning I left Hiroshi with Brian and went to my two classes (thank God they were back to back). Brian brought Hiroshi up to the university where we handed off just before Brian's classes. Brian hated it. He called it "playing Hiroshi football." I hated him hating it. But the worst part was not having any time to myself because when Hiroshi was asleep I had to study all the time just to keep up. After all, it had been a decade plus since I took sciences, and I wanted to do a good job of it. So I didn't read, I didn't write, I didn't sew, I didn't work out. I didn't do any of those things which are life-affirming for me.

I went to school, I studied, I worked, I ran the house. I got a staggering amount of practice at the number one survival tool for the nineties: establishing the highest priority. If I had any spare time I gave it directly to Hiroshi, because if he didn't get enough attention, he had a way of making himself the highest priority most unpleasantly and in short order. (Aunt Jean frequently related a story about telling my gran, her sister, that she wished she could chloroform her kids temporarily and put them on the shelf so she could get her work done. Gran said, "Jean, you'd never take them down!" And the wheel goes around.)

Lord have mercy, I had the blues. When my filing job disappeared, I was almost thankful—one less thing. Then of course, the money thing came back. I stopped paying my student loan. There was nothing to pay it with. And the government started laying off teachers. That's when I decided I'd better become a dental hygienist. I thought, "I'll start making $27 an hour, and I'll pay off that loan. They'll just have to wait." I was that stupid. I pulled a Scarlett O'Hara and decided not to worry about it. And that was easy because I was so bloody busy I didn't have time to worry.

Aunt Jean told another story about how her husband always criticized women for doing too much. They made work for themselves, he said. She left their infant with him one weekend (which in itself is amazing, a guy taking responsibility for his baby for a weekend in 1931) and when she got back, the kitchen reeked of urine. He'd hung the diapers up to dry without washing them. The baby had a bum like a grated beet. He'd saved himself some unnecessary work. *He* never said a word, and Aunt Jean certainly didn't criticize him, but she didn't leave the baby with him again either.

For my part, I would have liked a little more credit, since Brian and I seemed to be in competition. I had a little running mental speech: "Whaddya think, the shampoo just magically appears on the shelf? That the toilet paper will always be there, like the sun and the moon? Someone bought that toilet paper, someone noticed we were getting low and put it on the list and remembered to take that list shopping. Helllllo?! Someone pays attention to the little details and keeps the machine running smoothly. Someone does preventive maintenance, someone changes the oil, and fills the gas tank, and cleans the spark plugs so that the engine purrs like a cat—someone keeps this baby on the road! It doesn't happen by itself."

I actually delivered that speech, tactfully modified, twice. The first time Brian said, "I know," and the second time he said, "You don't have to cook."

I thought, "Oh, cool. I can stop cooking." But of course, as I mentioned before, I eat all the time, so periodically it behooves me to cook. Yes, we ate a lot of Kraft Dinner, cheap noodles and take-out pizza that year, but that gets expensive and hard on the complexion, so in between there had to be things like baked beans, scrambled eggs and bean sprouts, left-over vegetable soup or tofu, which Hiroshi miraculously loved. He was a picky eater; I deserved no less, my mother told me with glee. However, he would eat tofu raw, cold and in chunks dripping from his grubby little fists. Brian and I preferred something a little more flavorful than playground dirt—a lemon, garlic and tamari marinade, for example, or bottled Szechwan sauce. But I digress. The point was that I had to cook. If only for me.

See, that was the kicker. So many of the necessary things I did, I had to do for *me!* Brian would cheerfully make a pot of rice in his little two-cup cooker (which takes about thirty seconds to do) and eat it with an egg, day after day after day, till his intestines finally groaned for fiber. And certainly Brian didn't get spaced out as I did when the house got messy. And Brian didn't care if Hiroshi watched a lot of TV, having been raised on TV himself as a child. *I* wanted the clean house, *I* wanted the real food. *I* wanted the kid to read, and paint, and draw, and run run run by the ocean and in the park. And if Brian happened to benefit because I wanted those things, he wasn't about to say so.

"Why do I always feel like I'm doing more?" I would whine to my friends (who happened to be women).

"Because you're doing more," my friends would patiently explain, which irritated me no end, because the last thing on Earth I wanted to do was work on my "relationship." Spare me! Having spent the entire previous decade heaving with romantic turmoil (pain, marriage, more pain, divorce, more pain—ugg!), I felt I had done my time. I wanted Brian to be like water: essential, but for the most part, simply there, a perfect silky fit against my skin. I wanted to come away clean. I did not want to lurch along like a train, one coach banging against the coupling bolts of the next. I did not want to pull him down the track, puffing and blowing and worst of all, steaming.

How different are the perceptions of men and women! While sympathetically agreeing that I worked too hard, Brian simply didn't see why it should follow that he was responsible to step in and save me. Which absolutely nailed me to the floor.

Tofu With Taste/Tofu With No Taste

Tofu, God bless it, has no taste. It is, however, much like a sponge, so you can lend it whatever taste you like by marinating slices in a bowl. My current favorite marinade is:

1/4 cup soy sauce
1 tablespoon cider vinegar
2 teaspoons sesame oil
1 teaspoon sugar
crushed garlic and grated ginger
1 tablespoon Louisiana hot sauce (or whatever you've got that's piquant.) Tabasco will do, but refrain from using a whole tablespoon.

While the
slices of tofu are changing character in the marinade, cut up vegetables:
broccoli, baby corn, onions, celery, carrots, mushrooms, whatever, and the more the merrier. Stir fry in a little oil. Fish the tofu out of its sauce and cut it into fingers over the vegetables.

Then take the remaining marinade, add
a scant teaspoon cornstarch and
2 tablespoons water, and stir neatly. When the time is right (that is, when the vegetables are done to your personal idea of perfection), make room in the bottom of the pan to cook this marinade sauce. Stir vigorously to prevent lumps. Make sure the cornstarch is cooked before coating all the vegetables with the sauce—raw cornstarch is a disgusting thing. (Jo knows.) *Voilà!* Your supper is ready! Sprinkle with
sesame seeds and eat over
rice.

Some people loathe the texture of tofu, in which case there is no point in infusing it with taste no matter how exotic. If by some bizarre twist of fate you are called upon to feed persons of that persuasion, and all you have at your disposal is a block of bean curd, take refuge in the knowledge that tofu disguises well. To illustrate:

Cook a pot of
rice, one of the stickier varieties. Cut

assorted vegetables rather smaller than you would for a chunky stir fry. Sauté them to your satisfaction in a big frying pan or wok. Crumble your
tofu into tiny rice-like bits over the veggies. Add the pot of rice to emphasize your point. Heat well throughout.

Now there are two methods for adding flavor to this hash. If you like curry, there are lovely jars of paste which can be scooped out and sizzled around with the veggies a bit. If you prefer a liquid form of flavor, like Szechwan sauce or anything based on soy sauce, you will achieve best results by adding the flavoring last and mixing well.

Serve with chutney, a salad or both. Do not mention the tofu, which after all has no taste.

ELEVEN

I'm not making this sound like a lot of fun, am I? It wasn't. Good thing we didn't have a car because once again, I found I appreciated my time sitting quietly on the bus to the university, all by myself, doing nothing. Good thing we lacked internal combustion, because that meant that instead of rushing out of the apartment, strapping Hiroshi in the car seat and zipping to the supermarket, I had to wheel out the stroller and toddle to the store.

Hiroshi would be eager for a run, because that was still a new skill for him, so he'd laugh, and then I'd laugh, and I thought my heart would burst as I watched his heavy knit sweater with the engines racing across the bottom, the sweat pants and the little sneakers bouncing down the street in front of me, weaving from one point of interest to another. My big boy! Baby no more.

And kids don't hurry, so I wouldn't hurry, and I'd tell myself, "You're doing a good thing for your child. Take your time. This is the most important thing you could be doing right now." And of course, while I didn't factor it in to my calculations at the time, that was a good thing for me too, because I'd breathe deeply again, and all the right healthful kind of thoughts would start circulating: love, joy, appreciation for my good life and for Hiroshi and the beautiful world we live in.

My great-grandmother used to tell my mother a story about travelling west in a wagon train when she was a girl. They wanted to get where they were going before winter, of course, and on Saturday night they had a meeting. Half of the people wanted to stop and observe the Sabbath. The other half pleaded extenuating circumstances; they wanted to press onward. So the group split. By the next Saturday night, the first group had caught up with the second. That Sunday, they all rested.

I must have heard that story a hundred times. Was I able to benefit from this shining parable? No, not I.

A friend of mine gave me a wonderful Jin Shin Do massage/treatment and told me to go home and take it easy for a while. So I went home and made mashed potatoes, Spanish baked green beans and meatloaf. Then I did the dishes, organized my school notes and mopped the floor, all while I was planning how I was going to take it easy. By the time I got around to taking it easy, it was bedtime and I sank into my blankets like vanilla into whipping cream. Sleep just folded over me like a big white cloud.

These were the good things: I was doing well in my courses, and that was a triumph because while I had managed to come back to university and excel in the arts, I still felt intimidated by the sciences. Seems I spent my twelve years of public education (which I loathed with an enduring passion) convincing myself I was stupid and the next twelve discovering I wasn't. Gotta like that. Also, although it had been years since I'd enjoyed a comfortable cash flow (probably since high school when I lived at home and amused myself with a part-time job before I piled up a lot of obligations and living expenses), I felt quite good about learning to squeeze the orange a little harder. However, I distinctly remember buying coffee from the vending machine at school, so I obviously hadn't reached the peak of penny pinching I'm at now!

And Hiroshi was a source of wonder, of course. So odd, to be learning everything, absolutely everything from scratch—that gravity pulls down, that day follows night, that reaching for the electrical socket causes your mother to scream. How he delighted me, English major that I am, with his precocious pleasure in words which was apparent from his first lisped syllables.

He would choose a word for the week, and beat it to death. "Yank" sent him into gales of laughter, "hack" made him squeal with delight. A few months later, he'd choose something sophisticated, like "either" and tack it onto everything for style: "No oatmeal either." "No mama either." "No bedtime either." I was totally charmed when he began quoting from his story books; when he began making up his own stories, bliss pickled my brain. I have always been entranced by his love of words, and that talent was just emerging during the fall that I buried myself in sciences.

And that about covered the positive aspects of my life. I was not having a good time. Chemistry was okay, but it certainly didn't ignite me as literature courses did. Biology was just a grind. As I said, I was tired all the time. To my grief, the old existential angst came back. In the morning, the news brought tears to my eyes, at least until I'd had a coffee—after that I seemed to be able to support it better. Aunt Jean, living an hour away by bus with her daughter, Katherine, was dying of old age.

"I'm going downhill fast," she told me.

"You're going downhill fast, and I'm rolling a rock up the mountain," I said. "A long way up, downhill fast, what's the point?"

"I'm winding down, and Hiroshi is just starting up."

"If you're winding down, and Hiroshi is just starting up, I must be in the middle, spinning crazy like a top!" We laughed, but it didn't do a thing for my perennial problem with *raison d'être*. Life is hard and then you die. Oh goodie.

One morning I was playing "wash the car" with Hiroshi on the kitchen floor (that is, he washed the car, I washed the floor) while listening to a special radio report on children's rights violations. I have a problem with pictures. They get into my head and I can't get them out. That's why I don't watch the news on TV. When words alone will throw me to the floor, why make it worse? When the announcer described how little children are tied to the backs of camels because their shrieking makes the animals race faster, I saw my own son. I saw the flashing sand. The echoing laughter of bearded, robed men placing their bets throbbed behind my temples; Hiroshi's screams ripped me, lightning behind my eyes.

I thought, "I have this good life, which is quite hard enough, thank you very much. Am I to say, 'I'm okay, my son is okay, it must be okay?' I am so concerned with my mean little, narrow little life, all alone stone, rolling my rock up my niggardly little molehill. What right do I have to be so lucky, while others are not? What right have I to laugh, and break my bread, and praise God's fullness while someone else's Hiroshi lies broken and bleeding? And what right do I have to be so damn unhappy, when I am one of the lucky ones?"

I thought, "Each day I listen to the news, in variations, but what do I do to make my world better? I'm applying all my energy to taking courses I loathe in the hope that some day I personally will be wealthy. I have a foster child in Colombia simply because I cannot bear to think that I'm so poor that I have nothing to give away. I mail him $27 a month. That's less than I spend on cigarettes. I have this baby. I'm trying to be a good parent to the baby I'm directly responsible for. That's all I do. I am selfish, ineffectual and puny. And I'm exhausted." Then I plunked Hiroshi in front of the TV, opened the window and had a cigarette, because as I said before, there's nothing like trauma of any kind to make me want to smoke: candy is dandy, but cigarettes are even quicker than liquor.

When we finished our courses in December, Brian and Hiroshi and I went over to his parents' home in Vancouver for Christmas. We created a pyramid of paper wrapping and came home with a shit load of non-biodegradable plastic probably assembled by child laborers in Chinese factories, and then we had to find a place to store it all in our tiny apartment. On this festive note, I fell into 1992.

What-To-Do-About-Christmas Cookies

Okay, I know I'm not the only one who feels this way—maybe we should take a vote. What do you say, folks? How about we start having Christmas every *second* year?

It's not that I don't like Christmas. If that were the case, there'd be no problem; I'd just say, "Bah, humbug," and that would be that. But actually, I love Christmas. I love the pretty lights, I love good food, I love carols, and I love giving presents. It's just that I get carried away, and all of a sudden it's not fun any more. It's commercial, it's tawdry, it's tiring and I just want to take a hot bath and go to bed.

I already have a busy life. How the heck am I supposed to fit in something as *time consuming* as Christmas?

One thing I do like to do is make these cookies. They make a nice present, they make a treat to pull out when you have visitors, you can take them to a party. They get better with age (citrus peel is like that) and I feel it's perfectly acceptable to bake them in early November and leave them in air-tight containers in the freezer until I need them. I'm sure that's what Christmas cake was invented for: to cut down on December baking.

And they taste Christmasy. Feeling Grinch-like? Pull out a cookie. Dip it in coffee. If anyone asks, say, "Christmas? I *had* mine." So there.

Mix:
1 cup honey
1/2 cup brown sugar and
1/4 cup butter
Grate the zest of
2 oranges and
2 lemons. Call me picky, but seriously, I'd go for organic fruit if I were you. Just the thought of pesticide, wax and artificial color being grated into my cookies kind of turns my stomach. Combine zest,
2 eggs and the honey mixture.
Now mix up the dry ingredients in a separate bowl. That would be:
4 1/2 cups white flour
1 cup ground almonds
2 teaspoons baking powder
1/4 teaspoon salt
1 teaspoon cinnamon
1/2 teaspoon each ginger, nutmeg and cloves

Add the dry ingredients to the honey and butter in four stages, a quarter at a time. When the dough is well mixed, add
1 cup whole almonds. Divide the dough in half. If your dough is very sticky, flour it for easy handling. Put each lump of dough in a clean plastic bag to prevent drying out. Shape into rectangles about 1/2 inch thick. Chill for a couple of hours, or overnight.

When you're ready, heat the oven to 350°F. Take the dough out of the bag and cut into long rectangles, like biscotti. Space an inch apart on a greased baking sheet and bake for 15 to 20 minutes.

When the cookies are cool, you can glaze them if you like a little extra sweetness. Make the glaze with:
1 1/2 cups powdered sugar
1/4 teaspoon almond extract
1/2 teaspoon vanilla extract and enough
milk to make the glaze a little runny, enough to pour smoothly but not too quickly off a spoon. Do yourself a big favor: add the milk by the teaspoon instead of pouring straight from the bottle, as I always do. Drizzle the glaze in zigzags across the cookies. When the glaze hardens, you can freeze the cookies and wash the dishes.

TWELVE

And then it got worse. Way worse.

My body revolted. It began with bad gas that came and went and didn't seem to have any connection to what I ate and when, but I stopped eating anyway. I felt like I was walking around impaled through the solar plexus by a telephone pole. Some days I had spells so bad that I could hardly move. Even on good days I was sick. I slumped at the table after I got Hiroshi to sleep at night, thinking that if I sat in the right place, maybe I'd do homework, kind of automatically. Of course I began to get behind.

Another horrible thing happened gradually. I went up to the college where they ran the dental-hygiene program and signed up to let a student practise on my teeth. I thought this would be good exposure for me, since after all, this was supposedly my career of choice. But in exchange for clean teeth for free one gives hours and hours of one's open-mouthed time. By the time one's last bottom quadrant is cleaned, the first top one is dirty again—that's how long it takes. But that wasn't all. I went in there thinking, "Oh, this is cool! I'm going to be doing this!" and every time I left I felt more and more discouraged.

It wasn't the work itself, you understand. Frankly, I don't see a lot of difference between scrubbing toilets, putting things in alphabetical order and digging around in someone's mouth with a mini crowbar, except that the tools for the latter are more expensive. A right-minded individual can find *satori* in the most boring chore, I am told, and one shitty little job is much like another. It wasn't the work itself. There were two things.

First was the depressing number of years of training it was going to take me to actually be a qualified, money-making dental hygienist and how demanding those years were going to be. I wanted to have time for Hiroshi; I wanted to *be* with Hiroshi, not pick him up from daycare at ten to six and bring him home and put him to bed! And I still wanted another baby. That much I knew for certain.

Second (and this blew me away), all the student dental hygienists were the same—and I was not like them. I had plenty of time with my jaw cranked open to think that observation over; it was truly odd. In spite of the pastel uniforms, these women did not *look* the same—yet on some level they were virtually interchangeable. It was as though they were all made by the same manufacturer, or maybe they each had a life produced by Disney (coming out on video cassette soon). There were girls of all shapes and sizes, different hair styles, different nationalities, and I thought encouragingly to myself, "Once you get into a nifty little astro-suit, you'll look just like them! You'll be fine." But I couldn't imagine it. I told myself, "Once you've been cleaning teeth as long as they have, you'll have that same pleasant, ditzy, vacant aura." Like elevator music. Then I was terribly afraid that was true; dental hygiene would vacu-suck my brain.

I told myself I was imagining things, but when I timidly brought up the subject with Shirley, she said, "Oh yeah. Some professions are like that. For example, almost all physios wear sensible shoes."

"Maybe they need sensible shoes for their work," I said hopefully.

"They wear sensible shoes at home too."

I fought with Brian. I can't remember why, but I do remember screaming, "You feed me shit and then you're surprised when I throw up on you—what do you think I am, a walking garbage disposal?" He didn't speak to me for a week.

Hiroshi started throwing temper tantrums. He always was an emotional sponge, but also he had propitiously reached that stage in which the infant realizes there is some connection between cause and effect, and becomes extremely frustrated when he cannot always make things happen according to plan. In short, Hiroshi was angry because he couldn't control his universe. "So are we all," I told him grimly.

I went to the doctor about my stomach, and she sent me for tests. I drank a lot of barium and I lay like a pink prawn on spinach—ready to be nuked, in my green medical gown under the huge X-ray machine.

My ribs stuck out and my baby-stretched skin hung down in flaps, and I felt totally insignificant and ashamed.

Half of me believed that having a kid was the best thing we ever did. But the other half believed that people like us, like Brian and me, should be sterilized at birth and leave the procreating to the doctor/lawyer types. Yes, and all the poor peons should rise up in protest and commit suicide, leaving the more "successful" members of society with a huge body-disposal problem and the incentive to use up the Earth's resources faster by creating robots to do all the creepy little mind-numbing jobs only the already brain-dead or the desperate would take.

And I knew it was my own fault, that I was lying there under that unforgiving machine, costing the Canadian medical system money, and that this never having money was my own fault too. A wrong turn here, a misstep there. And certainly this was not what I expected from myself (this ineffectual flopping around like a skewered frog) when I was growing up. I come from a long line of productive members of society. Who could be more "productive" than farmers? But then, perhaps after all I was keeping the family tradition, because farmers never have any money. It seems our society does not value people who feed people. At least not with monetary acknowledgment. And money is everything in our society. Right?

My negatives showed no intestinal abnormalities.

I dreamed that I went for a head X-ray and there was something wrong with my head. I woke up and thought, "Oh great. It's all in my head. *Cut it off!!!*"

Dental Despair Fudge

The beauty of this fudge is that under normal circumstances, you will have almost all the ingredients at home, but you probably won't have whipping cream. So you will have to make a special effort to remember the whipping cream, and get out there and buy it. In other words, you can't decide you're depressed and you deserve fudge at 11:30 PM. Unless you live near a convenience store and have access to a baby-sitter, you must have a premeditated depression. This is for serious consolation.

1/4 cup butter
1/4 cup corn syrup (or Roger's golden, or honey . . . but honey makes a stickier fudge)
1/2 cup whipping cream
1 cup brown sugar
1 cup white sugar
5 tablespoons cocoa

These ingredients are for purists. Others can add instant coffee or omit the cocoa and add vanilla or throw in some nuts just before scraping the fudge into the pan.

Heat all the ingredients in a heavy pot. A Dutch oven is good. Let the fudge sit at a soft boil for moment. Then take it off the heat and let it cool for five minutes. Butter your pan. Set up your beater. Get something to read. Then beat with the electric beater until you think your beater is going to give up the ghost. When the motor begins to labor, and the fudge is folding over on itself, it's ready to pour into the pan.

There. Do you feel better?

THIRTEEN

And then it got even *worse*.

I had to drop my courses, not only because for the first time in my life I was going to fail and because I was too sick to go on, but also because I absolutely could not imagine myself applying those sparkling stainless-steel picks to enamel. I simply couldn't picture it, and without the picture, I couldn't see my way.

Still, I thought if I could only pull myself onto an island, I could rest for a moment and stand up with at least a portion of my dignity intact, and figure out where I was going. Instead I got a letter from Collections regarding my student loan. They wanted the balance of my account paid up. They were not prepared to negotiate. Too bad, Scarlett.

I'm not sure to this day why Student Loans did not contact me before turning over my account to Collections. They allowed the requisite number of months to pass without receiving a payment and that was that. Do I blame them? Certainly not. I owed them money. I blamed myself.

How could I have incurred that kind of debt load without a means or a hope of paying it back? Granted, I had not known my monthly payments would be half what my rent was for ten years but you'd think a person would look into little details like that when she was borrowing such a big lump of cash. How could I have imagined that my creditors would patiently wait because I was having a personal crisis? How could I have put the whole thing out of my mind? What had I done? What was I going to do?

At the time I was practically suicidal. I would cheerfully have killed myself, but I simply could not bear to leave Hiroshi. How dare I abandon him in a world which I could not cope with myself? But to kill him first was more than I could even imagine in any concrete kind of a way. How would one go about it? And what a thing to do to Brian! I'd have to kill him too, God bless him. Furthermore, my mother had long ago extorted the promise from me that because she'd lost her father so early and her husband too, she must be allowed to die before me. My hit list was becoming unmanageable. I had just enough sanity left to laugh, but no more.

Oh, I was ashamed of myself! And to drag a child into the business on top of it all. How could I have been so irresponsible? Because, you see, Hiroshi was the crux of the whole problem. I had owed money before and always before I had paid it back. I went to work, wherever work was (and there *was* work), and I paid off my debts. But this child! I wasn't free to go flying off to the Northwest Territories on a whim any more. Not to mention the hiring freeze in the oil patch. To put Hiro in daycare, support myself and pay my student loan totaled more than I could make. Wages went down, rent went up. I couldn't dump the kid on Brian; he had student loans of his own. He would have to go on welfare, and then we were back where we started, costing the taxpayer money, because we had chosen to have a baby.

The long and the short of it was that we should not have had that child. Naturally I should not have got pregnant, but cleverer people than I have got pregnant without intending to. I didn't feel too bad about that. However, I supposed I should have had an abortion. That would have been the responsible thing to do. But that thinking simply made me mad! How could I deny my son!? All that was good and light and sweet! Surely something is wrong with a society which would say I should not have had my son. Yet why should I expect the taxpayer to support my right to have a baby, or my right to go to university?

Why should Ms. Average, Shirley for example, with three kids of her own, on her own, struggling with a mortgage, paying fifty percent taxes on everything she made, including her child-support cheques—why should she be expected to donate toward my education? And welfare? Our social programs are supposed to provide a safety net, not a playtime trampoline for the feckless.

So maybe I should have given my baby up, to someone more likely to be able to support him. Everyone knows how hard it is to adopt these days, and plenty of diligent types who waited until they had the means to have a child found they waited too long to conceive their own. Did these people not deserve my beautiful boy much more than I? And what follows then? That only rich people should have babies? Shall we measure out their little lives, pay by the pound?

Then I kicked myself for all the bad investments I had ever made: the small piece of land which I bought with Daddy's legacy at the very pinnacle of the real estate market before it crashed. The house, which I abandoned to my ex-husband when I left him, and good riddance too. The education which was so much fun but ultimately more useless than a Christmas tree at Easter. All these things that I worked so hard for—and none of them could be applied to paying off my student loan!

Round and round and round I went. But no matter how I whacked myself on the head, I still owed $15,000 to the government. So eventually, I was driven to attempt logical reasoning. Let's face it. I had the boy. I wasn't about to give him up. I doubtless wasn't going to kill myself. I had nothing Collections could take that I wouldn't cheerfully give them (the ten-inch, black-and-white TV? My cooking utensils? Brian's grandparents' rocking chair? My ten-year-old computer?). They were more than welcome to my overpriced piece of land, and while they were at it, they could help themselves to my ex-husband's house.

I would gladly make payments till Hell froze over if only they would accept what I could give but Collections was not interested in making any deals. They wanted $15,000 cash. I did not have it. I simply couldn't pay. So what was the worst thing that could happen? In this enlightened age they couldn't throw me into debtor's gaol. They couldn't take away my son. I felt like a piece of shit but, when I got right down to it, on the list of stupid things I'd done in my measly little lifetime, the student loan was not necessarily the stupidest. And certainly I wasn't the first or only one to default on a student loan. I just hadn't thought it would happen to me.

True, I felt the schmuck for ripping off the government but then again no more than Brian Mulroney ought to feel, to say nothing of Mila with her $100 haircuts. What I really felt bad about was stiffing the middle class—the people who pay the bulk of the taxes by going to work, day after day, week after week, with their noses to the grindstone and their shoulders to the wheel. The taxpayers' dollars sent me to school, and while I'd throw peanut shells at the government any day of the week, I never meant to knife the taxpayer. I hoped that someday, I would make it up to the public: that my contribution to society would outweigh what I'd so thoughtlessly taken out of the general pool.

And so I resolved to file for bankruptcy. But when I finally came to this decision and phoned my mother to confess all, she reminded me that I owned stocks in her farm, which is a company, and that if I declared bankruptcy those stocks would have to be declared and given up, and she for one did not wish to co-own her farm with the government, or anyone else.

"And," she said with dignity, "we pay our bills." And I of course dissolved into yet another tidal pool of tears.

Well. To make a long story short (and the shorter the better, as far as I'm concerned), my mother bailed me. At thirty years old, when you'd think a person would have developed a bit of self-sufficiency or sense, or even both, I had to get my mother to pay out my student loan. I agreed to make small monthly payments, probably for the rest of my life, at six percent interest, which was what the bank was prepared to give her, instead of twelve percent, which is what the bank wanted from me. And Mom supported me fully in my desire to be Hiroshi's primary care-giver while he was under five, and gave me permission to make that my priority for the present. All that affirmation for $100 a month and the renewed promise to fill her basement with firewood on my annual summer visit.

What can I say? I felt grateful, certainly. But I had all the dignity of a gutted fish and I felt about as clean as sparrow droppings on a Chevrolet. And I was far too sick to eat.

Virtually Instant Meals

Well, friends, when I stop eating, it's pretty bad. I mean, I love my food. But here's the thing about kids. You may be sick, you may be sorry, but you've got to feed them, whether you feel like cooking or not.

So here is a short list of virtually instant meals. And if you have any additions or ideas, I'd like to hear from you.

1. Eggs. Blessed is the mama whose children like eggs, for she will always have a supper up her sleeve. Nothing is faster than scrambled eggs with toast. Crack an egg or two for each person, depending on their sizes and ages, add a teaspoon of milk for each egg (just splash it in; measuring is out of the question) and a snort of soy sauce. Mix with a fork. Cook on medium.

2. Grilled cheese sandwiches. Preheat the oven. Lay the bread out on a cookie sheet, cover with slices of cheese or butter and parmesan. If your kids eat tomatoes, slice those on top. Burning the cheese is the kind of thing that always happens on days when you need a fast supper, so take preventive measures: set the timer for four minutes.

3. Vermicelli. It cooks faster than spaghetti. While it's cooking, open a can of tomato sauce, cut slivers of tofu into it and heat it up. Serve with grated parmesan if you have it.

4. Nachos. Dump a bag on a cookie sheet, cover with chopped olives, red peppers, green onions, cheese, or whatever your family likes. Pop in the oven. Set the timer. Open a can of tomatoes, dump in a bowl large enough that you can ravage the tomatoes with a knife. If you have time, spice the tomatoes with chili, cumin, coriander, cayenne, garlic powder, salt, and/or minced onions. Call it "salsa." If you have an avocado, mash it with lemon juice, mayonnaise, chili powder, salt, and pepper. Call it "guacamole."

5. Baked potatoes. Scrub a potato for each person you need to feed. If the skins are thick, prick them. Nuke until cooked; the time varies depending on the efficacy of your microwave. Put grated cheese, butter and salt on the table.

Now, a proper mother would serve each and every one of these meals with vegetables and dip, and fresh fruit, so as to provide a balanced meal. But, I ask you, would a proper mother be in this position? Or maybe the question should be, "Is there such a thing as a proper mother?" You tell me.

FOURTEEN

It takes a very determined masochist to maintain prolonged periods of hand-wringing or self-flagellation when one has a child in diapers. Moaning and deep regret are all very well, but one's friends become weary of that kind of tripe pretty quickly. And I've had a goodly bit of experience recovering from doing stupid things.

My ill-fated marriage probably tops the list. The day my friends and I piled into a car driven by a guy I *knew* had been smoking dope is right up there on my top ten list too—from the back seat, we watched in horror as we slid off the road onto the beach with a nasty thump. I've boiled pots dry, missed planes, given away my Corgi toys, and as for apologizing, I've had so much practice pulling my foot out of my mouth that I could host how-to seminars on the subject. Yes, I am an experienced fool. So I survived my student loan crisis. But I got very thin.

I have never been what one would call a fat person. After my father died and before I discovered cigarettes, I put on quite a bit of weight. Voracious as a locust, I simply never stopped chewing. My jaws just kept clacking. Maybe I wanted to make myself into a monument, huge and immutable. Confirm my existence. With Daddy gone, one could never be too sure. The universe was shifting around rather a lot, in my opinion. Anyway, I gained weight and I didn't really lose it until I started smoking less than a year later. I've been slim ever since, so when I stopped eating in January, I didn't have much of a shadow to lose. By spring, I looked as though my nearest and dearest relations were sticks.

Brian was sweet to me, or at least as kind as he could manage to be as he struggled to complete his last semester at university. The best thing about Brian has always been that since he didn't want me telling him what to do when he grew up, he wasn't about to give me advice. As far as he could see, Hiroshi was okay and I would live—that was all that mattered. By the time Hiro was one and a half, Brian had completely accepted the model of the universe which placed Hiro at the center with all bright lights orbiting around him.

Once again, Shirley found me employment. I began cleaning her house three hours a week in theory, but in fact it took me all day because I brought Hiroshi with me. Her real estate agent hired me too, but she was a single woman with an immaculate and expensive place, so I left Hiroshi with Brian. Once a week I wiped all her clean surfaces and did her ironing. It was very restful, very pleasant, in that it was so quiet and all I had to do was work.

With that income I made my monthly payments to my mother. Government child-tax benefits bought groceries, Brian covered rent and hydro. About twice a month, I took the bus into the country to see Aunt Jean. Her daughter, Katherine, began to employ me for odd jobs, just as Aunt Jean had done. That money paid for taking Hiroshi to the swimming pool once a week, with coffee and a snack afterwards. Although my aunt died a few months later, I continued to work for Katherine sporadically. I could not allow myself to grieve too much for a woman who died with relatively good control over her body and mind at the age of eighty-eight. It doesn't get much better than that. But I missed my auntie, and spending time with Katherine was a comfort as much as a source of income.

We didn't have any spare change but as long as the basics were covered, money wasn't a big hassle. We were no worse off than before—in fact, better, without my tuition to save for or pay. The real problem was self esteem.

Jo's Golden Rule, which I have taken as the Eleventh Commandment for many years, says, "Never underestimate the insecurity of another person." Just because a person looks like she knows what she's doing doesn't mean she doesn't quake with self doubt at 3:00 AM. This adage was supposed to keep me from judging people and from comparing myself to others, because it doesn't matter how many toys a person's got, if she feels like offal, she's not winning as far as I'm concerned. You never know how someone else is *really* doing, better or worse; it shouldn't matter anyway. The main goal was always to love others and myself, and to try to walk right, which has nothing to do with anyone but me.

But I couldn't cough that attitude up. I couldn't stop comparing myself to others and coming up the loser. My self-hatred was stuck in my gut like a hairball. I kept looking at other people and feeling like a fuck-up. I should have known better than to have a baby before I had a good job.

Striving to be happy is a huge pressure. How can one succeed? One can never finish—graduate, get a certificate, and carry on, a happy person ever more. I decided I was not going to try to be happy. Better to strive to survive.

And the days inevitably rolled by. I did the dishes, I washed the diapers, I went to work and I took Hiroshi on excursions to the park and the beach. Hiroshi and I read a lot of books and painted a lot of pictures and made a lot of towers out of blocks. I nursed my stomach as much as I possibly could and at night I slept in my cocoon. I believed I'd never catch up on my sleep.

In the spring Brian graduated, at long last the proud possessor of a physics degree. It was a real triumph for him, and with all the love in my heart, I wanted to honor and mark his passage. I invited all his friends to a celebration; I planned a sumptuous feast. I spent four days making preparations while Hiroshi plucked at my elbows and whined for attention around my knees. The plywood plank we used for a desk and table was to be absolutely laden, groaning with food. I planned to have a turkey with all the fixings, sunflower seed stuffing, gravy, mashed potatoes, sweet potatoes, creamed corn and green beans stir fried with Japanese vinegar and sesame seeds. I would put out beet pickles and green pickles and for the vegetarians, a huge pasta salad with olives, three kinds of cheese and garlicky garbanzo beans. There was going to be a Waldorf salad and a green salad with two kinds of homemade dressings and rice (of course) for Brian. Then for dessert I made butter tarts, frozen pineapple delight and florentines.

I did everything I possibly could do in advance. The night before the party, Brian had to work and I stayed up until the wee hours of the morning, teasing delicate almond cookies off the pan and icing them with pure chocolate.

When I finally went to bed, I had a dream. In this dream, my sister-in-law was everything I wanted to be: capable, independent, strong, positive. She was apparently single, but she supported herself and her children, and she participated in a political group for women which was making a real and positive contribution to the world.

"Yes," said a voice in my dream, "and her son is a genius too!" I thought my jealousy would leap out of my throat and burn her. Then I looked at this person, this object of envy, and realized she'd lost a lot of weight. In fact, her skin had that flaky, papery quality of someone very old or very sick. With a shock, I realized she was suffering from anorexia. I grabbed her by the shoulders, shook her and cried, "Eat! You *must* eat! You are worth the food you put in your mouth."

When I woke up, I was sobbing, and the more bitterly I wept, the deeper I gulped air into that place in my belly which had held my pain for so many months. When I finally got up to blow my nose, I found the lump in my gut had dissolved. I took a very small piece of paper and wrote, "I feel guilty because I'm stupid. I feel guilty because I'm not successful. I feel guilty because I can't cope." Then I ripped it into tiny pieces and ate it with Durkee's Louisiana Hot Sauce.

"Goodbye to you," I said, "and don't come back."

The next day I celebrated. I put on my party dress. I drank a lot of cider. I held hands with my sweetie and kissed my son. And I ate from every dish on the table.

Three Kinds of Salad Dressing

1. Creamy Dressing

I have a problem: I love creamy dressing but I cannot bear the thought of a raw egg. That is my excuse for eating Caesar salad in restaurants where I can pretend that the egg bit hasn't happened. I do, however, have a recipe for a creamy dressing that does not call for a raw egg.

Blend at top speed:
3/4 cup vegetable oil
1/4 cup apple cider vinegar
1 heaping teaspoon miso
2 - 4 garlic cloves
Season with:
curry paste or herbs: **tarragon, thyme and savory** or **basil, oregano and thyme.**

Yum. But you have to get the blender out. And wash it. Ugg. Not so with

2. Dave's Dressing for Avocado and Tomato Salad

Shake in a jar:
3 tablespoons light soy sauce
3 tablespoons oil
1 teaspoon Dijon mustard
1 tablespoon red wine vinegar
pinch sugar
freshly ground pepper

Do not limit yourself to avocadoes and tomatoes. This dressing goes well with lettuce and broccoli and it makes a great tofu marinade too.

Easy. But

3. Plain old soy sauce and freshly squeezed lemon is even quicker.

FIFTEEN

It took me a very long time to get used to the idea of *just living*, without some kind of goal to be pushing toward. Very odd. It was the first time in years that I didn't have homework hanging over my head. I'd get to the end of my Hiro-day and think, "What should I be doing now? What should I be doing now?" Kind of like the last twitches of a hanged man.

We were in a resting period. Brian applied for the teaching program but the quotas were filled and he wasn't accepted. We were both relieved. We'd had enough of school, vicarious or otherwise. Then, by a stroke of luck, Brian started working more just as his student loan payments came due.

Of course I was still busy. I had a temporary new plan: instead of striving toward a career as a means to make more money, I decided to focus on needing less of it. This, I thought, would do for the moment, until I could think of something better. I found that approach almost the equivalent of getting a job, both in the amount of money I saved, and in the time and energy I spent.

I started in my kitchen. I made my own bread and did all our baking. One of my friends belonged to a food co-op and I invested in a sack of dried kidney beans, another of navy beans, two sacks of rice and one of popcorn kernels. These stocks were very reassuring to me. I thought, "At least we won't starve."

It takes time not to waste food (unless you live with a real Hoover). Someone has to pay attention to what's in the fridge and make sure that things get eaten up before they go bad. It takes time to organize menus, so that the beans are soaked before they're needed. I invented an absolutely delicious meatless bean soup, which has to be the cheapest meal on earth. You make it with navies cooked with bay leaf, onions and a little garlic. When the beans are very soft, add marjoram, thyme, soy sauce and a wee bit of olive oil. Very simple. Very tasty. If you bake a Half Hour Pudding in the oven at the same time, using whole-wheat-flour dumpling batter poured over boiled raisins, brown sugar and spices, you end up with complete protein, a filling meal and a warm home which smells deliciously of cinnamon and clove. Very energy efficient, very healthy, very *good*.

I did these things, and hundreds of others as well, from making my own cards and stationery, to walking instead of taking the bus; from cutting my own hair to making my own yogurt; from mending what was broken to shopping at the Salvation Army. If I couldn't find something I needed in the second-hand stores, at garage sales, or by any other scavenging method, I used a technique which is rapidly becoming accepted by the general public as more and more people rise up in protest against rampant consumerism. This marvelous method of redistributing stuff and keeping junk out of our landfill sites is called "putting out the word." Simple: tell everyone what you're looking for. Eventually it will come to you. Say "thank you," or "You're welcome— glad to see it put to use," depending on whether you're giving or taking, and everybody's happy because we all have an excess of Stuff.

I was discussing this phenomenon, this Explosion of Stuff, with Katherine one afternoon as I helped her purge her closets. I myself haven't had two cents to rub together (more or less) for about ten years, and yet I have a whole apartment full of Stuff. For the most part, I didn't buy it and Brian certainly wouldn't. (He was a minimalist trapped in partnership with a pack rat; adding to our Stuff was not something he would purposely do.) Most of what we've got was given to us, and what I did lay down cash for was almost exclusively second-hand. And the reason we've got all this second-hand Stuff is that other people didn't want it—they had more than enough Stuff.

Katherine said people started to get a lot of Stuff just after she got married in the early 1960s. Before that, when couples tied the knot their communities co-operated in starting the new family off with whatever could be rustled up in the way of cast-off furniture. My mom, as I mentioned, was born during the Depression, so she remembers getting one dress at Christmas and that was her church dress for the year. The year after, it was her school dress. The year after that she would naturally have outgrown the dress and it would become someone else's work dress. Mom also tells stories about when she and Daddy were first married, and how they had to scramble for cash. Katherine, my aunts, they were all the same. Then suddenly, boom! All this excess Stuff.

It doesn't really do us much good. Yes, I am truly, deeply grateful for automatic washing machines. But for the most part, Stuff doesn't put food on the table. It doesn't put clean water in a cup. It's Stuff. It came out of the earth and it's going back to the earth—a double whammy. We rip it out of our planet's guts and call it natural resources, and we fling it back as garbage. Violence. A kind of borrowing that's about as helpful as lending your toothbrush to a street person. You wouldn't want it returned.

As a friend of mine said, "It's a good deal—but for whom? Not for the Taiwanese worker in the factory. Not for the planet. If not for the people and not for the planet, then it's not a good deal for me."

The thing is, once you get started, it's hard to stop. Because fax machines exist, businesses have to have them. If you're looking for work, it's imperative to have an answering machine. And because the general public does not wear old clothes, there's a limit to how old one's clothes can look before one begins to stand out in an unpleasant way. Certainly if you're looking for work, it is important to look good. And God forbid if you happen to be ugly or scarred or old and looking for a job. We're a shiny little culture and appearances have got us by the knickers. We've whiter-than-whited this planet to death. But we look good, oh yes we do!

Of course, if we stop consuming, we'll put people out of work by the score. And of course, we *do* stop consuming because we *are* out of work by the score. Or maybe some of us have got something better to do than work to make money to buy things we don't need. I like to think that might be true. Mind you, it isn't a fear of not having Stuff that causes me to worry about the future—it's a fear of eating dog food in my old age! And the fear of eating cat food for breakfast tomorrow drives me to work today.

So although I felt better physically, I continued to obsess about the future. Sarah, who also graduated with an English degree, would phone me up and we'd have a discussion loosely known to both of us as "career of the week," a brainstorming session wherein theoretical possibilities and limits of potential forms of employment were considered, hashed over and discarded with alarming frequency. With my little part-time jobs, I made enough money to get by and go out for a latte once a week, but it wasn't a lifestyle I considered to be a permanent solution. I still figured that eventually, I would get out there and find "real work," whether that required retraining or not. I felt very much on hold.

While I was in this mood, my co-worker at my ex-place of employment as a file clerk went on holidays for a week, so I covered those five days of work for her. A part of me still strongly felt that I should be working more, or harder. Paying for my sins, perhaps. I said to myself, "Someday soon you're going to have to go back to work full time. Let's just see what it feels like." The work itself wasn't bad. It amazed me how much easier work was than looking after children, even with staff cutbacks and the pressure cranked up and up and up. However, being away from Hiroshi so much didn't feel good to me and arranging baby-sitting was a nightmare.

In my desperation, I ended up making a very serendipitous call to an acquaintance who, I heard through the community grapevine, was thinking of setting up a daycare. She could not in fact help me with my immediate problem but as we were chatting about the pull between going to work and staying home she asked me, "If you could do whatever you wanted to do, what would that be?"

"Right now?" I said.

"Yeah, right now."

"Well," I said after some deliberation, "actually, if I could do whatever I wanted to do, right now, I'd keep on doing what I'm doing. I'd make enough money to get by, by hook or by crook, but for the most part, I'd just be home with Hiroshi."

"So," she said, "what's the problem?" While I watched all the pretty lights going on (*Bing!*) in my head, she continued: "You sound impatient with this phase of your life. You sound like you feel you should get on with it. In fact, this time while your children are small and at home and they need you is very short. Once they're in school, they're gone from you forever. This time, because you're in it, feels like infinity but I'm here to give you the gift of perspective. This is a very short time. It will soon be over."

Then, like an angel, she hung up, and I felt as if my fairy godmother had just gone *whoosh* with her wand and layered everything with a thin film of sparkle.

It's not everybody who gets to do just what she wants to do!

Zucchini Loaf and Applesauce Muffins

(Making the Most of Your Excess Stuff)

When I say excess Stuff, I usually mean *things*, but come fall, a person with good contacts will find herself swimming in zucchini and apples. It's wonderful to be on the freebie list, and my friends love me because all good gardeners hate to see produce go to waste. The apples are no problem because you can sauce them and the sauce can be frozen in one-cup containers, but zucchini is more of a challenge. After you've had it in ratatouille, sautéed with tomatoes and onions, baked with crumbs and parmesan, what are you going to do?

Start here:
Preheat the oven to 350°F and grease one loaf pan. (Actually, to make this energy efficient, you should double this recipe and bake two loaves, so you'd better grease two pans.)
Soak
1/4 cup poppy seeds in
1/2 cup orange juice
While you're doing that, combine the dry ingredients:
1 cup white flour
3/4 cup brown flour
1 teaspoon each baking powder and baking soda
1/2 teaspoon salt
zest from one orange

Now, in the mixing bowl you intend to use, beat
2 eggs with
1/2 cup sugar. Add
1 cup grated zucchini and
1/3 cup vegetable oil

Add the poppy seeds and juice, then slowly add the dry ingredients, and mix until just combined. Pour into the loaf pan and bake for about 65 minutes.

When the loaf has cooled, glaze with **1/4 cup sugar dissolved in 1/4 cup orange juice.** The glaze is essential because there is so little sugar in the loaf.

Now, as for the applesauce, you can make cornmeal muffins. Soak:
1 cup cornmeal in
1 cup water
Add:
1 cup applesauce
1/2 cup oil
grated peel from one orange
1 egg, and
a little more than 1/4 cup sugar
Mix with:
3/4 cup brown flour
1/2 cup white flour
1 teaspoon each baking powder and baking soda

Bake at 350°F in muffin tins for about 20 minutes or until done.

SIXTEEN

After that psychological jump start, it was not a big step to realizing how good my life really was. We had all the crucial bases covered: we lived well, we ate well, we slept safely at night. I had always been so afraid I wouldn't be able to provide Hiro with "the good life." Ironically, beyond the most basic essentials, what he needed most so far was happy, healthy, caring parents: difficult to come by, but cheap.

Where Hiro was expensive was in lost wages. Every child is different, and some thrive better than others in daycare. Hiro wasn't a daycare type. Like both of his parents, he didn't like groups, nor did he have the least interest in other children. I knew in my heart that being at home and making a home for Hiroshi was the most important thing in his whole world, a thousand times more real than Suzuki piano lessons, private play school or spiffy clothes from expensive boutiques.

For the first time, I felt fortunate that I'd neglected to get myself a career. If I'd had the capability of making a whomping big wage, I would never have had the courage to stay home. I'd have felt compelled to work. And these days, "full time" does not mean forty hours a week. A salary and benefits require bringing work home at night and going in on Saturdays, staying late and applying for promotions you might not really want because if you don't, you might appear disinterested and We Can't Have That.

I phoned up Sarah and gave a speech: every day we don't have to be in the rat race is a blessing. Every day is a bonus, that we can put off signing up for the Full-Time Job—and fifty percent income taxes, RRSPs and the big house with a private room for every person. Cutting the lawn on weekends to keep the place up, or there goes the neighborhood and property values go down. Dealing with the plumber and the mechanic and sitting up with the sump pump when it rains so the basement doesn't flood. And having to buy those ugly platform shoes because that's what everyone is wearing at the office now and it wouldn't do to look different. It's bad for company image, you know.

We should be patting ourselves on the back, I told Sarah, for having pulled off another day on the fringe. We ate, we drank, we slept in a warm place and we managed to play hooky from the flock, not for the sake of playing hooky, but because time is precious and we know how we want to spend it.

Once I'd accepted the concept of staying home with Hiroshi and working part time as a viable lifestyle alternative, I began to revel in it. I started to see my way of life as a positive direction, a chosen path, rather than a dismal trek through "the valley of the losers." I had a lot of advantages if I could bring myself to look at it that way: cleaning and sewing gave me the flexibility to center my energy on Hiroshi, and I had the time to be responsible to the logic that we need to consume less for the sake of the Earth. I had time to make cookies instead of buying them in little plastic trays, in wax-coated paper, in celo-wrap. I had time to be kind to my neighbors. All my old beliefs rose up to the surface with force—that life with fewer possessions, fewer distractions and fewer commercials would be a good thing for our hearts and our planet, and clearly for my son.

Occasionally I'd have a fear relapse but I was much better. One day while I was worrying about the future (I thought of it as a dirty little habit, like picking a scab, or biting one's nails), predicting the decline of the western world and imagining how much worse things could and probably would be in the future, it occurred to me that someday very soon, the present would become "the good old days."

I imagined Hiroshi asking me, "What was it like in the good old days when Canada still had social assistance and we always had enough to eat?"

"Well, son, you see we didn't realize those were the good old days; we were too busy worrying about things getting worse." *We lived in the good old days, and we didn't even notice them passing!*

Having a sense of where we are in history helps me, and in this century, historians have got a lot better at focussing on ordinary people and what the big changes (such as the Industrial Revolution, the Great

Depression and the Fall of the Roman Empire) meant to individuals as well as to countries and political systems. Life has always been a struggle. That's not likely to change.

Here's a strange detail that stuck in my mind and surfaced as a reminder to rejoice. Even in this century, in fiction written either about or during the two world wars, authors talk about having a shortage of eggs—about recipes for eggless cakes, or about having one egg and saving it for the baby. Well, Brian loves eggs; an egg is comfort food for him; he especially likes to eat them gently poached in his noodle soup. Because this is so and because I love him, I never let us run out of eggs. Not only that, but we don't have just any old eggs; I buy beautiful, orange-yolked globes from free-range chickens, because they're just so much better than those nasty little factory-produced farts. These delicious eggs became a symbol for Brian and me, an antidote to fear.

"There are eggs in the fridge," was our password: *we are still okay, Brian and I, for now. Life is still better than good. These are the good old days.*

Eggless Cake

(For Depressions, Recessions and Vegans)

Actually, I read somewhere that in most baking, a tablespoon of soy flour and another of water can be substituted for an egg, so maybe eggs aren't as essential as I've always taken for granted. I've accidentally left them out of muffins before with passable results. And this recipe (from my mother, who got it from *her* mother) doesn't call for any egg replacement and it's moist and delicious.

Boil in a pot:
1/2 cup raisins
1 1/2 cup water
pinch salt
1 cup brown sugar
Five minutes will do the trick. Add
1/4 cup oil (Butter's better if you're not a vegan.)
Cool about 5 minutes. Add spices:
3/4 teaspoon cinnamon
1/2 teaspoon nutmeg
1/4 teaspoon each clove, mace and allspice
1/2 teaspoon vanilla
Add drys:
1 1/2 cup whole-wheat flour
3/4 teaspoon baking soda
1/2 teaspoon baking powder

Mix until incorporated. Pour into a greased square pan. Bake at 350°F for about a half an hour or until done.

While this cake doesn't really *need* sweetening (like I don't really *need* my third slice), it is scrumptious with cream cheese icing, which you make by blending softened
cream cheese with
icing sugar and a little
vanilla. Thin with
milk as needed.

Vegans and those unfortunate souls who are allergic to milk can top the cake with a sticky brown-sugar icing, made by boiling

brown sugar
corn syrup and
olive oil (wee bit) almost to the fudge stage. Very gooey and decadent.

SEVENTEEN

And what about Hiroshi, while all this was happening? He grew. That's what kids do. He got more sophisticated, he developed a kind of reasoning and it was eerie to witness the manifestation of my parenting techniques. One day I bawled him out soundly for hanging out the window (we did live on the third floor; it was a serious misdemeanor) and after indulging in a little cry, Hiroshi sat there and listed his good qualities for me—everything I'd ever said.

"I'm very smart."

"I have a beautiful smile."

"I'm very polite."

Et cetera. I was most impressed. That's a double-edged sword though. For the unpardonable sin of turning down the wrong aisle at the drugstore, I called myself stupid, and then I had to listen to Hiroshi call himself stupid for a couple of weeks before I got him trained out of it. You have to be so careful what you say. Harder still, you have to be so careful what you believe, because restraining yourself won't stop what's really inside from coming out, nor would you want it to, ultimately. What you say may be the flour in the cake, but what you believe is the flavoring, and the flavoring is supposed to flavor, right?

So if you want your child to have good self esteem, the first thing you must do is foster it in yourself. If you want him to believe the world is a beautiful, worthwhile place, so must you. If you want him to know life is ripe with meaning, you must know that for yourself, down to the bones of your body where your cells are made, so that every new cell vibrates with purpose, and sparks against the ions in the air, and triggers the molecules in the food you prepare, and maybe then your child will eat your meaning in his peanut-butter sandwiches, and maybe he will breathe it, inhale it, while sleeping, when you kiss his smooth, warm cheek late at night. First, you must love yourself.

I didn't really worry much about Hiroshi. He was so obviously okay. So incredibly beautiful. So present in his day, such a little boy, playing with his cars or stalled on the street by a construction zone. I had to laugh. Ms. Anti-Internal Combustion had a son who loved anything on wheels. I gave him every opportunity to play with dolls. He had his choice of the traditionally feminine play things. He had zero tolerance. He didn't even start drawing people until he developed an interest in knights and armor.

People always talk about the terrible twos. I didn't experience them. But you know, it is often easier to talk about difficulties than pleasures. I mean, how many ways can I tell you Hiroshi was the light of my life? Every day I appreciate the fact that I have running water (having once lived without it), but I don't write home about it.

Hiroshi was becoming less demanding in some ways. There were fleeting moments when I could actually read, or do chores by myself. But more independence also meant more getting into mischief. I didn't want Hiro to be thwarted but I also didn't want him to be spoiled. I sometimes felt like I was always saying no. "No, you may not wash your car while I'm washing the floor if you don't wring out your rag. No, you may not fling flour across the room, à la catapult, while I make bread. No, you may not clean the toilet with toothpaste. No, No, No. For God's sake, let's go to the park where I don't have to say no!"

Age two is when the mama begins to get some of her self back. Separation starts to happen. I emerged. Rip Van Winkle: "Hey, where was I? I had a life, didn't I, once upon a time?!?" One suddenly realizes how little time one has to oneself, how seldom one is alone. Oh yes, some kids nap till they're five, but guess what: *some kids don't*. Hiroshi woke up at six and went to sleep at seven-thirty. If he napped, even for ten minutes, he'd be up another hour.

I kept telling people it was a long day. I'd been telling people that for a long time, you know, casually, conversationally, "It's a long day," and then all of a sudden, one day it hit me. *"Holy shit, this is a long day!* It just goes on and on and on. I am on duty twenty-four hours and this kid only sleeps ten and a half hours, and in between, this is a long day! No wonder I'm grumpy. No wonder I'm tired. This is a long day, Mama, and I don't mean maybe."

It was about that time that I pretty much stopped watching videos altogether. I never was much of a movie fan, but Brian was, and renting a flick was something we occasionally used to do together. But nobody wants to watch a bad movie and a good movie enfolds you; it takes you under its softy little wing and absorbs you. Then after two hours, it spits you out (pit-oooey), half digested, and you rub your eyes, and Hey! Wait a minute! All your free time *sans* child is used up. It's time to go to bed, bud, or you will not be a cheerful and pleasant mama tomorrow.

I wanted to do more than one thing in my precious evening time. I wanted to saunter around savoring it. I wanted to create something lasting: a poem, a costume, or a project. I often wanted to talk on the phone, have a real conversation without interjections ("Take your fingers out of the VCR, you're going to get an electric shock!"). I wanted to enjoy a snack; I wanted it all laid out, food, cutlery, drink, salt and pepper. I wanted to eat it from beginning to end without standing up once. I did not want to wipe up any spills. I wanted to sit perfectly still for at least ten minutes. And I wanted to read, all by myself (just to prove I still could read silently to myself) before I went to sleep—but it couldn't be anything too engrossing, or I might be tempted to stay up too late.

I had two solutions to the last problem. I read *Pride and Prejudice* over and over and over. I totally ruined it for ordinary consumption by using it as a sedative. And I read recipe books. I love to read. I love to cook. I love to eat. But I have never stayed up until 4:00 AM to finish reading a recipe book. I have never been so excited by a recipe that I could not get to sleep. Ergo. Perfect bedtime reading.

Reading cookbooks fueled my passion for cooking. I made a virtue of necessity, and more and more used the production of the daily meal as a creative outlet. I had to have one. The urge to cultivate genius does not disappear with the placenta; it simply takes a leave of absence and re-emerges, like a calcium deficiency which makes one twitch in one's sleep. "Hello? I'm still here, your creative genius. Do something about me!"

Mind you, I wouldn't necessarily say the food got any better. Mealtime was more interesting, maybe, but experimentation did lead to some dismal failures. My croissants, for example. I prefer to forget them. I learned to make exotic, labor-intensive foods: the little Chinese pork dumplings with finely chopped vegetables spooned into round dough moons, crimped, fried and steamed. Spring rolls, with spicy filling encased in water-softened rice-paper wrappers. Poppy-seed braid with marzipan filling, steaming from the oven. And while I often paused in the middle of a huge mess, having exhausted both Hiroshi's patience and my energy, and howled aloud, "Why am I *doing* this?!!" in actual fact, I believe I could have chosen worse by way of entertainment. One way or another the meals had to be made. And culinary art does not gather dust.

When I was in Athens many years ago, I was befriended by a girl named Fanny who had left her family because her father abused her. She got a job in a cookie factory and made enough money—just—to have her own place. She in turn rescued me from a real jackal and I stayed with her for a while in her barren, dark basement suite, giving her the money I would have spent at a hotel. Four walls. Cold linoleum. Austere washroom. Two sleeping bags and one wooden chair. Fanny's clothes in her suitcase; my backpack propped up.

The kitchen area had a counter, but no stove or fridge. Fanny had a little platform of bricks set up so that a two-cup pot could sit over a flame which she made with cotton-batting balls doused in some kind of fuel—alcohol, I think. Fanny bought it in plastic bottles at the supermarket. I hoped she knew what she was doing. With this arrangement, Fanny would make a bowl of instant soup, or a cup of coffee. How often I have thought of her, oil on canvas, "Fanny in her Kitchen," humming to herself as she moved about preparing our simple repast, the comforting and nourishing hot food that made the bread we ate with it taste like a meal. This was her creative solution—her safe place.

In my own kitchen, the same feelings prevailed. Safety. Wellness. Goodness. When visitors came, it was my pride and pleasure always to offer them food. In this way I celebrated abundance. In this way, I made myself one with the thousands who break bread together as a symbol of peace. People all over the world press food on their guests as a sign of generosity, acceptance and welcome. This is a universal message: "We have food. All is well. Eat."

Pork Dumplings

Pork dumplings require a lot of chopping if you don't happen to have a food processor. This recipe is adapted from the dumpling wrapper package. I buy the wrappers in Chinatown. I suppose you could make them but I'm not that masochistic yet.

The filling:
1 pound ground pork
1 large finely chopped onion
3 crushed garlic cloves
1 tablespoon sesame oil
2 tablespoons soy sauce
2 tablespoons grated fresh ginger
1 can chopped water chestnuts
2 grated carrots
2 finely chopped stalks of celery
1 egg

Combine the filling and place it by the teaspoon on the dumpling wrappers, which you then proceed to dampen around the edge with a little water to make them stick and crimp them together. They can be frozen just like that, to be fished out around 11:00 PM after watching something toothsome like *Eat Drink Man Woman*. Or you can cook and devour them right away.

Brown the dumplings in cooking oil in a heavy skillet. Flip them once and throw 1/2 cup or so of water into the pan. Cover quickly with a tight-fitting lid. The dumplings will be cooked through in about seven minutes.

Eat with
chili sauce mixed with
crushed garlic, or dip in a sauce made of
red wine vinegar
soy sauce and
grated ginger.

EIGHTEEN

What a strange thing parenting is! On one hand, the days go endlessly by, one after another, filled with chores, duties and (let's face it) drudgery. Half past four rolls around and you think, "Damn Sam, what are we going to have for supper, and how am I possibly going to get through another mealtime, clean-up, bath time, snack, tooth-brushing, story time till I reach (sweet mercy!) the last goodnight kiss?" And of course you survive it, day after day.

On the other hand, Christmas creeps up like Maxwell with his silver hammer and suddenly you find yourself up to your eyeballs in icing sugar, Smarties and gingerbread men, and you notice you've got your own full-fledged, walkin', talkin' little automaton, buzzing off a sugar high (around and around the kitchen, hollering, "Jingle bells, jingle bells . . ."). You stagger back in amazement and say, "Where is my adored infant son, the one I held to my breast and nourished there?"

Or you happen to see a new mother proudly parading around with her Snugli and her sweat pants and twenty extra pounds of maternity fat and deep black circles under her eyes, and you think, "That was me. But no more. I'm a seasoned mother now. Where did the time go?"

Hurry up and wait.

I wanted my second baby. My vision of my family was so real to me, that baby just had to be. Her empty space was a palpable thing. However, I did not want children more than three years apart. I could not see myself running through the infant obstacle course twice.

What!? To be rid of the diapers, the colic, the trips to the park. To be finished with felt-marker designs on the walls. To have passed along the strollers, the high chairs, the cribs. To feel the return of a healthy aversion to anyone under the age of two. To have a semblance of your life back, never your old life of course, but to be promoted to stewardship rather than acting as a full-time deity. To have moments, even days (!!!) off, if not free from worry, at least released from active care. And then . . . Whoops! Surprise! Here comes baby number two, back to square one, do not pass go, do not collect two hundred dollars, no, no, NO!

Don't get me wrong. I liked being a mother. But it's a very consuming job, particularly during the early years, and I didn't want to spread it out. Mothering was not the only thing I wanted to do with my life.

Then why bother with kid number two at all, you might ask? Because Hiroshi (or Napoleon, as it turned out) needed a sibling. And heaven forbid that the Emperor should ever do without a single little thing! (You didn't think you were getting an unbiased report on the loveliness of this child, did you? Why, I had friends, without children of their own, mind you, who thought he was a demanding, whiny little brat—I dropped them.)

So as the days crept by and we got closer to "forty weeks before Hiroshi's third birthday," did I resign myself to having an only child? Ummm, no. I'd have to say no.

I've noticed a trend. It kind of scares me. One way or another, I very consistently end up with what I want. This magical ability does not bring me instant gratification (that is to say, one tantalizing, titillating delight after another in succession). Rather, I tend to kind of float down the river, banging from bank to bank, exclaiming, "Goodness! This is just what I ordered. Only different. How odd!" (And while we're discussing it, I want it put down for the record that I'd like to die in perfect health in my sleep painlessly at a ripe old age well before my children.)

"Brian," I said as the moment of truth approached, "should we use a condom?"

"I'm not sure," he said.

"I am," I said. You'd think he would have had an attack of *déjà vu* at that point.

The funny thing was, I had so much desire around having a second child that I was afraid of regretting my wish. You know that saying, "Be careful what you wish for—you might get it." That haunted me. When I finally did get pregnant, it was Brian who did the welcoming.

Once again, I had a bad case of "What have I done!" *What if child number two was a psycho-baby? What if psycho-baby turned into horror-child? What if the fetus had the makings of a Bad Apple? What if he or she turned out to be the bane of Hiroshi's life?* In my more neurotic moments, I sighed to myself, "Life has been so wonderful, so beautiful. I hope I haven't done something to make it bitter for us all!"

Brian cured me of that quite inadvertently. We were lounging around in the bedroom. We had our futons side by side, so that we had wall-to-wall mattress (pillows, comforters, bears—it was wonderfully cozy!). Hiroshi was entertaining, bare naked, thin brown limbs and penis flapping, on top of Brian's trunk: "Ladies and Gentlemen, the Invisible Dance!"

"But I can still see you!"

"Close your eyes then," Hiro instructed.

Brian put his hand on my belly and said, "I guess we're going to be a family now." In that moment all my anxiety flushed away. *That* was why I wanted that second child.

But I did not think, (no, not for a second), "Oh, this baby is going to make my life so much easier!" Even in my sanest moments I knew I was about to double my trouble. I also figured I was about to lose all my hard-won spare time, at least for a while. (And I was right.)

I have a confession to make. I am a crazy woman for a list. It's what I do to keep my project psychosis under control. If it's on the list, then I won't forget that I wanted to do it, whatever "it" is. And I have all my lists graded: *Things I want to do today. Things I need to do soon. Big projects. Things I want to do before I die. Things I'd like to do, but hey, let's face it! we all know it's never going to happen.* Then I have all kinds of minor lists. *Things I want to buy at the drugstore. Books I want to read. Books I want to write. Movies I want to see. Gifts I'd like to buy people if I ever win the lotto.* When I'm feeling particularly spacy and unfocussed, I read my lists the way other people read self-help manuals.

Well, after Baby Q was conceived, I did a corporate takeover on the project list. I thought, "Life as we know it is about to change completely. Again. If I want this done within the next ten years, now is the time." And I went nuts. It was a nine-month productivity blitz.

I wrote and illustrated a book for Hiroshi, made underpants out of my old cotton T-shirts, organized all the notes on my fridge into a quote book and put all our snapshots in chronological order in a photo album. I created and typed out a collection of recipes for one-pot meals for a friend who was living in a tiny hotel room downtown with only a one-burner hot plate to cook on. I sewed a silky quilt for the new baby, an engineer's hat for Hiroshi and five finger-puppets, designed in such a way that the engine on Hiroshi's thumb pulled three cars on his fingers and a caboose on his pinky. I tutored a little third-grade boy who was having trouble with his reading, typed the memoirs of a woman dying of cancer and went to her funeral, filled my freezer with suppers for when the baby came, and made my mother a dress. And Hiroshi did everything I did, except not so well, and with incredible mess as a by-product.

I made myself so busy that when Mura was actually born, I kind of slumped to my knees with a grateful sigh.

In some ways I had more clarity during my second pregnancy. I knew that I wanted above all to be home with my children when they were small, and I bent all my purpose toward achieving that goal. Besides, this time I was well aware that by having a second child, I had effectively priced myself out of the daycare market forever. But we were blessed. I had an easy pregnancy. I was able to keep working right up to my ninth month, and Brian was experiencing a period of comparative prosperity at his place of employment. He was able to support us. Also, in the spring and out of the blue, I got a call from a real estate agent about the piece of property I had bought with my legacy money from Daddy. I was able to sell it—I took a real header, lost money big time, but the sale enabled me to pay off my mother, which took a big load off my mind. (All that anxiety over that loan and it was gone within a year. Why do I beat myself?)

So you'd think with all that good fortune, with all that "getting what I wanted," I'd have been ecstatic. Nope. I just kept going up and down like I normally did. Sometimes I think the sun brings us up, and PMS brings us down. Maybe it's all hormonal, no relation to outside reality whatsoever. Mind you, you're not supposed to get PMS when you're pregnant. Maybe I had PBS—Pre Baby Syndrome. At any rate, I did not receive the existential relief I had experienced when I was pregnant with Hiroshi. I kept looking forward to that, and it just never happened. Instead, I remained firmly rooted in my physical material world, preoccupied with making it through the day and down the list.

Bubble Mix and Playdough

(Yet Another Entry on the List of Things To Do)

Yes, here are two *more* things to do, but they're *good* things to do!

Make a huge batch of bubbles and gather up all your bubble hoops and head to the park. Homemade bubble mix is cheap and saves bringing yet another plastic container into the world.

Mix:
1/4 cup light corn syrup
2 cups warm water
1 cup dishwashing liquid
That's all there is to it. Off you go, bubble your heart out.

Now, supposing it's raining, or snowing, worse luck, and your children are climbing the walls. Making Playdough *will* occupy you (for about ten minutes), but after that, it should keep your kids out of your hair for a good long time.

In a heavy pot combine:
1 cup white flour
1 cup warm water
1/2 cup salt
1 teaspoon vegetable oil
2 teaspoons cream of tartar
Cook over medium heat until the dough thickens and begins to come away from the sides of the pan. Don't burn yourself, but if you can touch it and your hands don't get gucky, it's ready. Take it off the heat.

First activity: divide the dough between children and let them choose which food coloring they want for their dough. Food coloring stains clothes and carpets something awful, which is why some people prefer to add the coloring before cooking the dough. However, combining colors is really fun, so you have to decide if you can live with the mess or not. Fold the coloring into the dough. Add glitter or sequins if you like.

Second activity: play with the dough. Make roads for a game of cars and tow-truck, bury plastic dinosaurs and excavate them, sculpt the

Empire State Building, or roll the dough out and make cookies. At this point your kids should be playing independently. You may have coffee if you wish.

Playdough creations can be dried, but the thinner ones work best, like cookie-cutter creatures for example. The big lumpy space aliens don't dry so well in the middle. If you're making Christmas tree decorations, poke the hole for the string before drying, because if you try to do it after, the playdough breaks.

Playdough will keep for months in an airtight container in your fridge. The little bits that grind into your carpet last a long time too.

NINETEEN

Why are men and women so different? I used to think it was social-
ization. Having kids was, therefore, a perfect opportunity for
experimentation. But Hiroshi liked bright blue and cherry red and,
after wearing her brother's hand-me-down sweat pants for two years,
my daughter, Mura, took one look at a lacy, frilly little number I'd been
hiding in the back of the closet and hollered, "It's *pink! I want* it!" She
put it on and that was that; down the slide, through the dirt, rolling in
the grass, she turned that party-pretty an innocuous gray.

I've come to the conclusion that men and women are fundamentally
different. Which would be okay, except that we each think our own way
is better. And we can't communicate. Consequently women, who give
more, work harder, and want more from their relationships than most
men seem to do, become frustrated and bitter when men don't respond
in kind. And when our men don't respond to our giving, we're so
dumb, instead of saying, "Hey, well, that approach didn't work," we
just keep on grinding away, hoping one day he'll wake up and notice
that "Hmm, one of us seems to be making all the coffee here, and it
isn't me."

But of course he doesn't, because men don't (or else he figures that if
you didn't like making coffee you wouldn't be making it), and pretty
soon the giving turns to poison in our coffee pots, but we keep on
pouring, and next thing you know we're all swimming in a big sticky
pool of toxic waste, caffeine and honey, saying, "Hey! What happened?"

Okay, that's a generalization. Okay, already, so it's a great big warted monster of a generalization. All I'm saying is that while I was pregnant with Mura there seemed to be a large percentage of my friends in the process of splitting up, and consequently, I heard a lot of things like, "What a buncha useless tits men are!" (I don't know what their men were saying. I dread to think.) And while I cheerfully nodded and bonded and murmured, "Isn't that the truth!", Hiroshi would lean over in the stroller, look up at me from beneath his baseball cap with those big, round, black eyes and say, "What is a 'useless tit'?"

There is a fine line between observing what is so and creating the future.

I started to dream that I was leaving Hiroshi behind. I had this theme in several variations. I told myself, "You're worried that the new baby will separate you from your son." But I knew that wasn't quite it, because the dreams kept coming. Finally, I became impatient and spoke aggressively to my subconscious. "Okay, so I'm thick. Send me clarification please. I'm not getting the message." That night I had a very powerful dream that I couldn't remember but I thought, "I know what that means," stumbled out of bed and wrote *"Strong desire for psychic union coupled with the strong need for awareness, in order to avoid destructive patterns."* Then I woke up.

So there I was, up in the middle of the night, with the revelation in code that it was not going to be okay to stay stuck in my little patterns and cling to my little attitudes if I wanted to continue to have a real relationship with my man-son. What was I really saying, anyway, me and my coffee klatsch? That men are lazy, irresponsible and obtuse? That they leave the dirty work for women? That men are uniformly unworthy of respect by their very nature? Ouch!

And what was the message I was passing on to my son? That only as children are males acceptable? Maybe not even then? A penis cancels all, see? That we (not only Hiro and I as individuals, but the whole population) are inevitably doomed to be separated and polarized on the basis of gender?

I shuddered. That was not what I wanted. My desire was to have a good, long-term relationship with my son based on loving acceptance of all that he was and ever would be. I wanted Hiro to become a man, healthily separated from both his parents, comfortable in his manliness; a good man with both pride and humility.

I wanted Hiroshi (and all boys for that matter) to grow into adulthood fulfilling his whole potential as a human being. Yet without ever saying a negative word to Hiro personally, my blanket condemnations, so carelessly spoken, diminished his horizons, by vehemently deni-grating what he would inevitably become—a man.

I once knew a man: a middle-class, middle-aged, moderately successful, graying businessman. A product of our society—a misogy-nist. He had a daughter, a princess. His little darling. Beautiful. Intelligent. Charismatic. Maybe a lot like her daddy. Ambitious. Proud. But because she was a girl, he kept her down. Never dreamed of grooming her for a position in his business, as he would have done had she been a son. He hired her as a secretary in the summer. He introduced her to eligible young colleagues, married her off in flowing white and orange blossoms, demanded grandchildren. And in spite of the vastness of his love for her, his attitudes toward all other women had long taught her to expect nothing better—that she was his pet, and therefore exempt from his scorn—but only as long as she remained his pet.

In the same way, I was binding and crippling my son. Because I would not imagine, would not acknowledge the beauty and goodness of positive masculine power amidst what is not so beautiful, I was holding Hiroshi down. And I was ashamed. True, men and women are very different—but should this not be cause for exploration and celebration?

I felt my hand had definitely been slapped. I had the will to improve and the reason before me, embodied in Hiroshi—but how to move from anger and resentment to appreciation and acceptance? Especially with boxcar after tanker of past patriarchal abuses bearing down, flatcars and dome cars and first-class sleeping cars laden with present-day problems (count 'em while you wait: *"Domestic Violence," "Street Violence," "Child Support," "Workplace Equity"*) on and on, car after car, screaming down the track, thousands of tons' (and years') worth of impetus . . .

That's a lot to lay on one small boy.

I just wanted Hiroshi to have a chance to be a good man. Wanted him to have a chance to say, "No, I'm not getting on that train. There are other modes of transportation available."

I sat down with my pen and made a list of all the men I have ever admired. I was forgiving—I didn't ask them to be perfect. After all, I didn't expect my women friends to be perfect. But each of the men on the list had to have at least one quality that I admired. I ended up with thirty-seven names off the top of my head. I hadn't realized I knew so many good men.

Then I lay down beside my son, and gifted him from each of the men on my list: Fairy Godfathers, at Sleeping Handsome's christening.

From the first, intellectual fervor; from another, the ability to listen; from the third, religious sincerity; from the next, tenderness; from the fifth, passion and conviction; from the sixth, enthusiasm; from the seventh, a sense of humor—and so on, into the night. When I reached the thirty-seventh fairy, I pricked my finger on a spindle and fell into a deep, deep sleep.

The next day I was just exhausted. I brought Hiroshi down to the lawn in front of the apartment building where I could peer into the basement window at the washing machines, and sat there, sinking into the grass, while the sun poured down and our clothes went through their cycles. Hiro had his flag, a long stick with a yellow pennant and an "H" appliquéed on it. John, our super, came down.

"March like a soldier," he said to Hiroshi.

"I'm not a soldier," Hiro said, waving his stick over the grass with concentration and great diligence.

Everything seemed to be moving in slow motion, and I thought I could not possibly live in a more beautiful world.

Excellent (Gingerbread) Men and Women

To encourage good will between the sexes, add wets to drys.

Wets:
3/4 cup butter
2 cups brown sugar
2 eggs
1/4 cup honey
2 teaspoons white vinegar

Drys:
2 3/4 cup whole-wheat flour
1 cup white flour
1 1/2 teaspoon baking soda
2 teaspoons ginger
1/2 teaspoon cinnamon
1/4 teaspoon clove

Roll to 1/4-inch thickness, cut out into the shapes of little men and women and bake at 325°F for about 12 minutes.

Place in a cookie jar labeled "Domestic Bliss and World Peace." Eat lovingly, two at a time. Feel good? Charitable toward your fellow human creatures? Wonderful! Hold that thought and make it happen!

TWENTY

I think one of the reasons why the dream sequence for changing my attitudes toward men came to me when it did was that the baby growing in my womb was a girl. There was no doubt about that and I could feel her power within me. I didn't spend the same kind of time bonding with this fetus as I'd done when Hiroshi was in my belly. Having Mura inside me was like wearing comfortable silk underwear: luxurious, secret and complete. Yes, I had Hiroshi to keep me busy, but as well, this new baby didn't need my attention. Mura was contained in a way Hiro would never be.

Ask me how I knew all this even before she was born? Okay, I confess: it was just a feeling. Whether my belief in her independence made her independent or whether my intuitions were simply right on, I cannot say but she came out baked. She never was a floppy little newborn baby—she was self-possessed right from the start.

I labored with Mura on the only night Brian had off before a run of ten straight nights at work. Mom came to stay with us, and particularly with Hiroshi, so that Brian could take me to the hospital. We drove out at about 3:00 in the morning, and met my dear friend, Eileen, in the hospital birthing room. Because Eileen was childless and in her forties, I wanted to give her the opportunity to experience childbirth. (The best labors are vicarious.)

"This is not nearly as bad as last time," I announced, just before it got worse. I'm sure you've heard this description of childbirth: take your bottom lip in both hands. Pinch it as hard as you possibly can. Then pull it over the top of your head.

Fortunately, second labors are frequently faster than first ones. We were all done by 6:00 AM. I squeezed out a squealing, squirming baby girl, and she rested on my belly, and *there she was!* Wide awake, offended and holding her head high. Her limbs were sturdy and brown, her grasp formidable. There was none of this itsy-bitsy, so-helpless-little-critter stuff. Rather, I wanted to fall to my knees and thank Her Highness for the honor of having been her hostess for nine months, and plead for the privilege of taking her home.

I felt that if I closed my eyes and opened them again, she might be standing before me, giving me an imperious wave: "You're dismissed." That she had chosen me was an ecstasy which placed me next to the angels; that she was mine to hold was a glory past compare. Brian was similarly and instantly smitten and I had it from Mom that he came home and *hugged* her (an unprecedented event which he not only couldn't recall later but didn't believe he had co-operated in).

"You have a baby sister!" he hollered at Hiroshi.

When Brian returned the car, Mom drove Hiroshi out to the hospital. He came racing down the corridor in his sneakers and blue jeans, looking about three feet taller and infinitely more grown up than the last time I'd seen him only hours before, and leaped onto the hospital bed into my arms. My in-laws brought me sushi and orchids. The sunlight beamed in all sticky sweetness and goodness. It was my honey day. I lapped it up.

And the next day I had my tubes tied, on the grounds that if the worst came to the worst and we had to move back to the farm and grow a garden to survive, I could handle hoeing potatoes, but I didn't want to be popping a baby between the rows of carrots every spring like some old cow. Yep, while Medicare still covered it, I wanted my fertility curbed. No surprises five years later for me, thank you very much. After all the yearning and desire I had experienced for a second child, I reveled in the feeling of completion, the luxury of ending the procreating part of my life without a single twinge of regret.

And then I went home with my newborn baby.

★★★★★

I believe I wrote this chapter once before!

Did you ever wonder why there is so little literature out there featuring mothers of small children? I'll tell you! The job is so incredibly time consuming, repetitive and even boring, chronically fatiguing, brain blotting and mind numbing that mothers of small children do not usually write. (And then, as with labor, they forget what it was like.) Unless there is a nanny waiting in the wings, grunt and grind is about all there is to the plot line for approximately four years.

Here's an example of a-day-in-the-life. Hiroshi, who at three years was scared of the dark and could not yet reach the light switch, woke me up at six because he had to poop. I crawled over Brian (who would be just on the verge of falling asleep), turned the bathroom light on, stumbled into the kitchen and scrambled two eggs which Hiro ate while he watched mother's little helper, the VCR, and I stole a few more precious minutes of sleep with Mura at my breast. Got up when Hiro sat on my head, putting his foot in Mura's face. Slapped in my contacts, gave both kids vitamins, prepared a bath while listening to Hiroshi chat: "I'm glad you're friendly today. When I'm happy, you're happy. But when I'm sad, you're unfriendly. You're mixed up good and bad. I love you Mama—I like these pajamas. They're cozy!" Et cetera.

Stripped Mura of her stinky night diaper, washed her in the tub, cuddled her up and fed her. Good time for a story for Hiroshi. Ate a piece of toast, and put soup on to simmer for lunch. Dressed three individuals, made sure Hiro peed, found boots and coats and finally went out. (Leaving the home is always, always a challenge.)

"Chugged" down the street. (Hiroshi was in his train phase. "I know what God is. God is a passenger train, going to Granny's.") Deposited a cheque, bought groceries, picked up books from the consignment store. At home again finally, I put away the groceries and gave lunch to all including Mura (who was easy, being strictly on the tit). She fell asleep. ("Quick Jo, think! What should I be doing to make it easier when she gets up?") Special time with Hiroshi. Cleaned the bathroom together— Hiroshi did the bit with the brush. Cleaned up after Hiroshi.

When Mura woke up, we bundled up again and walked along the beach. This exercise was necessary to make the apartment quiet enough for Brian to sleep, the better to work all night. Back home at about 4:30, I let the kids wake Papa while I made supper. Ate together, fed Mura while Hiro watched Brian get ready for work, chatting vigorously all the while. Put Mura to bed, kissed Brian goodbye. Bathed Hiro, gave him a snack, brushed his teeth, read him stories, put him to bed. Deep sigh.

Cleaned up the supper things, had a bath myself, mended Sarah's jeans (five bucks a pop), read six pages, Mura woke up. Hushed her down. Took out my contacts: free fall into a deep sleep. One or two night feedings during which I was only semi-conscious.

Variations on same again tomorrow.

Is it any wonder that on stormy days we'd all go down to the sea wall and scream into the crashing waves? Literally howl at the foaming, boiling water? Mura, relaxed in her Snugli against my breast, slept through it all.

And where was Brian while all this was going on? That was the year of the horrible sleep thing. For as long as I'd known him, Brian needed a lot of sleep, far more than the average person. He was working so much that even on his days off there wasn't any point in switching over to day shift. The club where he worked was busy and loud; Brian came home vibrating any time between 3:00 and 5:00 in the morning. It took him a couple of hours to power down. By the time he was ready to sleep, we were up and making noise. One more kid raised the decibel level in the apartment considerably. He'd emerge grumpily from his cave in the late afternoon without having achieved REM state—and the kids would fall on him because they adored him to distraction.

How different are the roles of Mama Bear and Papa Bear. I slogged it out. I did the long haul and Brian came off like Mr. Fun, the guy with the tricks and the goodies and the toys. It was annoying, this "good cop" stuff, since I got to be the bad cop, but I wasn't jealous. I had worshipped my own dad, as my mother did hers. To dote on your father—that was the correct state of affairs; it gave me a feeling of all systems proceeding at "normal." Besides, the love I had for my children was incorruptible. No one could come between us and nobody could take them away from me. I had nothing to lose by my children loving their father and everything to gain.

Brian loved them differently than I did too. My love was ladled out in bowls of soup and slabs of homemade bread. My love was something that came from my gut to theirs. My life was blood and bones: mess, rigid structure and a lot of hard chewing. I felt huge. Immense. My children fed off me and I grew larger still. In my mind, I was all belly and tits, like a fertility goddess.

Not all of the ancient goddesses were kindly and nurturing, though. Some were arbitrary, some voracious, demanding sacrifice. I, too, could be quite awful; I could feel where the image of the mother who devours her young came from, and the expression "love you to death." I had almost too much power.

Brian, on the other hand, did not spread his love out on the banquet table like some huge Christmas tourtière or a suckling pig, and then stand there with his hands on his hips. His love was more like a coal that burned, lighting him from within. Something you couldn't see but that made him hot to the touch.

And he was totally and unequivocally biased. One day I picked up fish and chips from a recently opened shop downtown that Brian had taken the kids to and recommended glowingly. The food was terrible.

"How did you come to speak so highly of this place?" I demanded.

"It was better last time," Brian said, and paused. "The owner said Hiroshi had an astonishing vocabulary for his age."

"And that made the meat more sweet?" I teased.

"An astonishing vocabulary," Brian said. "Those were his very words."

Cute. Touching. Amusing. Still, I felt like Brian was sending postcards from Hawaii while I battled in the surf. I had been swept out to sea, too far for sign language; all I could do was wave. We lived in separate worlds.

*****

I found it hard to keep the house as clean as I wanted it to be, but if I told myself, "Housework isn't important," then how could I give myself credit for doing it? And I did a lot (whether it showed or not!). I found that the level of mess I was prepared to tolerate went down in proportion to the number of children I had.

Hiroshi definitely got to do more than Mura, and at a younger age. I let him play with the flour when I made bread, unwind spools of thread to create webs, and design forts with chairs and blankets. However after Mura was born and before Hiro got to be a real help cleaning up, there was a period where I couldn't even handle finger paint. It was just too hard to catch up, with two of them creating disasters and only one of me cleaning up behind them.

One day, another mother and I were chatting away about the merits of vinegar versus bleach in diaper-pail hygiene and suddenly I realized, "Oh my God! We're discussing cleaning solutions! Just like a TV commercial! Next we'll be comparing soap brands! Are we reduced to this?!!"

I remembered a fling I once had with a man (*boy!*) a few years younger than me. We took a bottle of hooch down to the beach and made love beside the driftwood with a big fat voyeur of a full moon sailing by. I was his "wild woman," his "love bite." That person, that self-same person was me! Whaaat happened!?

Most of the time I was too tired to remember anything about my other life. My present life overwhelmed all. Yet, although it sounds terrible and tedious to me now, actually all I had to do was do it. I was on a roll. In fact, when I had a moment to analyze my existence, I felt as though I was careening down a corridor (swiftly past all those doors that used to be there for me), wheeling down a steady, predictable path. I felt that I was going to do a zillion diapers, wipe a trillion tears, make a million meals, wipe a billion bums—and it would be fun. Eventually, I would get a job and make more meals, wipe more tears and pay dentists' bills, and after a time my kids would graduate and I would enjoy their visits home, and work some more, and dandle my grandchildren and then one day, I'd die, and it would have been fun, a regular slice, I wouldn't regret a minute of it—but that was all there was. A life totally focussed on the survival of my children and me; no possibility of ambition or contribution beyond sustaining my own immediate family. The day-to-day stuff was just going to consume me until I croaked.

Some say the work increases exponentially with each child. How would you feel if you had six? Ten? Thirteen? Some say it's the third child which slays you—you run out of hands just as your baby equipment is giving out and the house gets too small. Some say after three, it's no big deal, just one more baby. I wouldn't want to chance it. Aren't you glad you aren't Catholic? Yes. Yes I am. And I'd like to send out a salute to the grandmothers and my ancestors, who had no choice in the reproductive department. "Here's to you!"

I struggled. Don't you dare think I'm wimpy, or inadequate. I would feel so humiliated if you did. Even parents with resources like nannies and grandparents in the same city complained about the effort it took to stay afloat. It's not just that the grunt work is overwhelming and the hours are terrible. It's also that the state of being permanently emotionally engaged means that the circuits are busy, all of the time.

Furthermore, I don't know why this is but everything happens at once. The phone rings when the baby craps. The scones must be taken out of the oven at the same time as Hiroshi gets his finger stuck in the wind-up toy. One day I had Mura on a little blanket, airing out a red bum, when Hiroshi came into the kitchen and demanded a snack. The buzzer went off for the oven, I turned around and Mura had pooped and was preparing to make body paint of it, when someone knocked at my door and wanted me to sign for a parcel. With my dirty baby under my arm and a pen in one hand, I watched in horror as Hiroshi flushed a diaper down the toilet and water cascaded into the hallway. The oven buzzer was still ringing; so was the phone.

Living in the now? Getting the most of each shining moment? Don't make me choke! There were so many chores, so many interruptions, that I felt very accomplished just to be able to prioritize and focus: okay,

I'm going to do the floor, then change Mura, then the laundry will be ready. I never did fewer than two things at once: make supper and supervise kids, buy groceries and walk the kids. Meanwhile, in between distractions, which shining moment was I supposed to enjoy?

Frankly, I commended myself for the fact that I strove to appreciate those beautiful children. Mura nursing, her big brown eyes following her brother, whom she worshipped, around the room. Hiro telling stories to his granny on the phone: "Did you notice that I love you, Granny?"

"Brian," I said, "why do you have an egg carton in our bed?"

"That's a diesel engine."

"Oh, of course! Silly me."

In each day there were flashes of bliss, and I made a point of noticing them as they blipped by. I made a point of trying not to wish my days away. Happy? I was pleased if I was consciously "happy" five minutes between breakfast and bedtime. And yet, rocked in my blankets, enveloped in the utter peace of the night, I found myself praying, automatically, without thinking, "Thank you God for the blessings You have heaped upon me."

Still, there were also times when I thought I was going to go crazy, a pet trying to escape from a smooth, clear, glass bowl. And there were occasionally even darker moments when I wanted to beat my kids. No, I never actually did, but I'm not exaggerating. Now *there's* an ugly monster, the horror we have inside. Oh, we use those words in jest all the time, we mothers chatting at the park. "I wanted to smack their heads together." "I could gladly have slapped him."

We tell it, we make it normal, lighten it up, admit and purge but the feelings are real. But does anyone tell you, say, at pre-natal classes, to arrange a buddy system? With a back-up? A non-judgmental adult whom you can phone and say, "Come quick. I'm too angry. I want to hurt them." Someone who will know what you mean, who won't think you're a bad mother, who won't call social services. Someone you can call for respite. Some kind of a solution to the huge gray area between coping and committing yourself to the mental-health institute.

Show me a mother who says she doesn't know what I'm talking about and I'll show you an emotional leper completely out of touch with her feelings. Plus, it's generational. When I confessed my violent feelings to my mother (and very tentative I was about telling it, too) she said, "Oh sorry, honey, you got that from me."

"I did?" I gasped.

"Your father would never let me spank you for fear I couldn't stop."

So there you go. I discussed the need for a buddy with my parenting friends, and even went so far as to set one up, but did I ever call her? I didn't have the nerve. I called Brian, yes. But once when he was away, I hid under the covers with both fingers in my ears listening to the roar of my blood, unable to pick up the phone.

★★★★★

Hiroshi adjusted to Mura more easily than I ever expected. I felt quite proud of him until she got herself mobile and changed all that. She got into his toys. We put Hiro in Mura's playpen where he could play in peace. Mura leaned yearningly against the mesh netting until she finally made a hole big enough to squirm through. Then Hiro moved to the top of the bureau.

"Put her back in your belly," Hiroshi ordered. That was on a bad day.

On a good day he told me, "When Mura is bigger, she will understand, and when I say, 'Don't pinch!' she'll say, 'Okay Hiroshi,' and when I say, 'Let's play!' she'll say, 'Okay Hiroshi.' "

Actually, we may never achieve that enlightened balance of power. Mura adored Hiroshi but she simply would not be bossed. However, things in general went a lot better after we discovered "the birthing game." I bought the book with the photographs of real fetuses which I had enjoyed so much when I was pregnant with Hiroshi, and I read it aloud to him probably a hundred times. A few months after Mura was born, Hiro developed a game involving a pillow case which he would climb inside and we'd run through the events of labor. After much pushing and groaning, Hiroshi would be "born" and I'd lift him in my arms and exclaim, "A baby boy! Just what I always wanted. Oh I'm so happy, a beautiful, beautiful baby boy!" *ad infinitum* while Hiroshi smirked. He couldn't get enough. And thus he reminded me of his own miraculous nature!

And Mura? She had no need to remind me of her presence any more than the sun needs to remind me of its power. The kisses from the sun cannot be bought or earned. Also thus with Mura. Her smiles, her chubby arms around my neck were gifts randomly given, dependent on her whim. She was filled with healthy energy, physical joy. If she'd been a fruit she would have been a ripe blue plum: small, firm, common but also sweet, juicy and absolutely delicious.

And laugh! Mura was the queen of fun. Hiro had the words, but Mura had the motion. She learned how to make faces to get Hiro giggling almost before she could crawl. She was generous to a fault; those brown eyes would snap and sparkle and she'd be off to make enough mischief for herself and Hiro too.

Sometimes I would ask myself, why would anyone ever have two children? Why put yourself through those paces? And the answer is different from the one you give before you have that second baby. When you have your first baby, it's all so new, and like the blind man and the elephant, you think, "Oh, so this is how it is. So this is how children are." And even though you observe that all children are different and unique, you don't really believe that—you believe all children are like your child. Then you have your second, and she's so absolutely and totally different, you are rocked from complacency. An infinity of doors becomes possible by implication, rather than one.

Oh yes. When you have your first baby, you love him so much. You never knew there was a love like that and you can't believe you could ever love that much again. Then you have your second and Hallelujah! You double your love. Inconceivable—impossible—yet you love the second one just as much as the first—but differently. It stretches your heart.

And I have it from Mom that when you have grandchildren, that's when you learn to love the World-child, Every-child. It stretches your soul.

Peanut Butter Honey Balls

(Park Food)

Park food is low-labor, high-energy, portable food that is toothsome enough to work as a bribe when you need to extract your children from the park and go home. Children hate change. They don't want to get into the tub—they don't want to get out of the tub. They don't want to go out—they don't want to go home. (I'm no better: I don't want to go to bed—I don't want to get up.) After a lovely morning at the park, when the children have been too busy playing to consume their snacks, blood-sugar levels dwindle and all hell breaks loose. I've seen more than one mother leave the park with a screaming two-year-old tucked under her arm.

So! Park food. In a heavyish pot over medium heat combine:
3/4 cup peanut butter
1/3 cup honey
1/3 cup water
1/3 cup milk powder

Stir diligently or this will burn. When you judge the sauce to be thick enough to absorb 2 1/2 cups of dry ingredients, take it off the heat.

To make up the said 2 1/2 cups, use any combination of whatever you like:
coconut, oat flakes, graham wafer crumbs, wheat germ, fine bread crumbs
Combine with the peanut butter and honey.

As soon as the mixture is cool enough, make it into balls and put them in the freezer. The only problem with these cookies is that they will wilt in the heat, but if they are frozen when you leave the house, three hours later they will still be intact.

When it's time to go home, call five minutes. "Hiro. Mura. We're leaving in five minutes." Pop one ball in your mouth. This will give you energy for the fight. When you have finished eating, five minutes is up. Retrieve your children using the donkey/carrot method and peacefully leave the park.

TWENTY-ONE

And Brian?

There I was with my million-dollar family, two beautiful kids and eggs in the fridge, and I still had to find the flaw in perfection. I had to look around and go, "Hmmm, things seem to be going pretty good. Everybody is healthy. We've got enough grub. I've discovered the perfect recipe for fudge and I know how to make the ultimate hash browns. How shall I entertain myself? What can I pick apart? Oh hey! You over there. Father of my children. Why don't you step over here and do a half turn? Let me get a good look at you—yep, there's grist for the mill." There always has to be something to complain about.

Yes, Brian supported us financially and I was grateful. Grateful because I wouldn't have wanted to support him. Grateful because I wanted to be home with my children and he made it possible for me to get what I wanted. Grateful because he was faithful and honest and good. But every day, like a burning in my belly, I resented the fact that he had free time and I didn't.

If he wanted to hang out with his friends playing chess after work, he simply did. If he felt like going off somewhere in the afternoon, maybe to get a haircut or pick up a video, he put on his shoes and went out the door. Whereas if I wanted to do anything, even so much as step out for a quart of milk, I had to dress up those kids and drag them with me or chase them bounding down the street. If I wanted to do anything without the children, elaborate preparations had to be made. Yes, Brian would take them almost any time I asked him to but in his silent way, he made it almost impossible to ask.

"Nerves, girl, nerves," my friends urged in frustration. "Make him give you the real support you deserve." But the friends who said this were invariably single, having given up on relationships long ago themselves. I did not want to be single. And I did not want to be pushing and shoving and fighting. My friends who were in relationships simply nodded their heads: "I know what you mean."

I felt like howling, "Is this the way it's always going to be, from now on, forever?"

Oh, it's not easy. Or simple. The fact of the matter was that I knew it was my responsibility to ask for what I wanted, and I didn't do that. I also knew that I complicated matters by not wanting someone messing around in my territory—I liked having everything my own way, even if it meant doing everything myself. We lived in an apartment that was almost exclusively mine—everything about it screamed, "Jo." Brian's space was all interior and increasingly out of bounds to me. And of course you know what happens then! The more I hammered at his door, the thicker he made his walls. Oh, it's not easy. Or simple. And it's so painful.

I'm not talking about a cold spot of a couple of months here. No. This was a continuation of the situation we had created when Hiroshi rejected the bottle in favor of the tit. We embraced traditional roles and somehow, in the course of the years, it got to be "Jo and the kids." They were attached at my hips, glued to my sides, a bulky addition to my girth. Meanwhile Brian, loving parent though he was, somehow managed to retain his psychic space. And this jagged hedge between us over who did the dirty work and who got free time was the accumulated growth of years.

He said he still loved me. I said I still loved him. But I thought I was going to shrivel up, totally dehydrated, and crumble into a fine ash. Nothing would be left of me, but a baby-soft powder—poof! Gone for good. God knows how Brian felt, but I knew he wasn't happy. And how that hurt me, because I'd tried so hard to bring him so much of sweetness and light.

I didn't think we were going to make it. "Should I go or should I stay" is right up there on the top of the list of my least favorite marital games. And believe me, I've got a list. I decided to make my annual summer visit to my mother an extra long one.

It's not like I'm talking about something unique here. This dance floor is well ground down; this is a familiar battlefield. In fact, a male friend of mine who happens to be gay once said to me that couples fight over only three things: sex, money, and "I'm putting more into this relationship than you are!" Maybe the first two categories fall into the third. One issue. One world.

So are you holding your breath to see what miracle resolved my situation? Thought maybe there was something you could use, or apply to your own life? Maybe you've been there—maybe you're there right now, thinking, "This is intolerable. This is unbearable. What can I do? What should I do?" Well, I wish I could help you!

The fact is that in the four years since I took my trip home, no fewer than five of my friends have split with their sweeties over much the same barrel that I was bent over with Brian. I haven't been able to help them— other than to listen, that is, and ply them with homemade hot and sour soup and keep on saying, "Yeah, oooo, I hate when that happens!"

Mind you, don't you find one usually sympathizes with one's friends, male or female, who wish to leave their partners? I can never blame anyone for wanting to toss in the bed sheets—who knows what horrors they have to endure behind closed doors? Besides, other people's room-mates (whether lovers or friends) of either sex are totally repugnant to me. They all have such undesirable qualities. They're too fastidious, or too messy; they're too distant, or worse, they want to get cozy; they have no social conscience, or they're too righteous. And room-mates who cast their stuff behind them the way slugs leave trails are the worst. Even the thought of other people's food in little containers growing mold in my fridge makes me green around the gills. Let's face it, there are very few people I would actually want to live with. I can scarcely tolerate living with Brian, who barely makes a ripple as he passes through a room. (God only knows how he manages to put up with me.)

I went home and whined to my mother. Now, I have another confession to make. I almost always do what my mother tells me to do. I try to make it look otherwise, but I almost invariably take my mother's advice. Partly that's out of respect for her opinion. Partly, if I don't intend to take her advice, I don't ask for it. But also, as my sister kindly pointed out, I don't have the oomph to make up my own mind.

So I went home to my mother and asked for help. Then I took her advice. I stayed for six weeks. It took me that long to stop feeling mad.

*****

"I can't see my way out," I said.

"Give yourself a break," said my mother. "Get some emotional distance. Do you believe in miracles?"

"Yes," I said dubiously.

"Good," she said.

That was round one.

★★★★★

"Let go!" my mother said. "You're nagging him!"

"But I didn't say anything!" I said.

"You don't have to," she snapped impatiently. "Brian is very sensitive, very intuitive. He reacts to your vibrations, not your words. If you want to change his reaction, change your vibration. It's that simple."

"But why is it always me doing the work, even this?" I countered.

"Do you want to change the picture, or not?"

That was round two.

★★★★★

"Can you change him?" my mother asked.

"No, of course not. I know that! I'm not that stupid."

"Then you must love and accept him the way he is," my mother said.

"But Mom! It's not fair."

"Life is not fair," she said. "If you want fair, go buy yourself a rubber doll. Life is good and rich and full and very, very hard, but it is not fair. First love and accept him the way he is. Then you can decide if you want to live with him, as he is, or not. Because you can't change him. You can change the picture. But you can't change him."

That was round three.

See why I've got nothing to say to my friends? If I reeled off stuff like my mother fed to me, I wouldn't have any friends left!

★★★★★

The possibility of splitting with Brian and finding someone else never once occurred to me. For one thing, even the men in the movies who made me sweat and drool uniformly looked, talked and acted like Brian. He was the very model of the kind of man I always fell for. Why should I ditch him, when I knew I would turn around and pick the same guy again? Furthermore, my polling operations revealed that few couples were much better off. Like I said, a lot of people bite the bullet over division of labor, and if it's not that, it's something else. Relationships are "terrible hard work."

Apparently some people out there believe in Mr. Right, or even Mr. Better, but I'm not one of them. Nope. I figured my choices were to stay with Brian or be single. I did not want to be single! I did not want to be poorer than I already was. I did not think Brian would be much fun as an ex-Significant Other. I wanted my children to have a father—they saw too little of Brian as it was. Besides (and this is important) I could not picture myself as a single parent. It's not what I imagined or envisioned myself doing. Obviously Brian could be annoying (all people can be annoying) but there was nothing really wrong with him. He was a good man: honest, kind and true. One could do much worse than that.

That was what it all boiled down to for me. Did I want to be single or not? I did not. How romantic.

So I took my mother's advice. I decided there were enough spin-off benefits in having complete control of my domestic environment to justify doing most of the work. I decided to remember I do the things I do for me, because I want them done. I decided to stop measuring, and ask myself instead, "Is this okay for you?" I decided I would ask for help when I needed help, because I needed help and not because I felt (with anger and resentment) that Brian owed me. I decided I would ask for help before I reached Red Level Crisis Desperate Mayday Stage. I decided I could accept and respect Brian in spite of his imperfections and give over the judging of him to God. I decided that was a lot to work on and that working on it could be a lifetime's work. I decided I did not want to go through deciding again.

Then I made a list of all the things I liked about Brian. It was surprisingly long. I reminded myself that I loved him. Then I remembered how true that was.

And I got my miracle. After six weeks, I went home and unpacked my bags. I was able to be happy—not every day, mind you, but most of the time. Do you know, we didn't even talk about it—why I went away, why I very nearly didn't come home? I waited for Brian to bring it up, but he's not like me. He doesn't need to talk. That's something he does for my sake. I decided I didn't really need to go over it all again.

A couple of months later I asked him, "Did you know I almost left you, this summer?"

"Yeah," he said. Long pause. "I knew you'd be back for your books."

And that was that. Nothing changed. Everything was different. Not the kind of experience you can pass along to a friend.

Hot and Sour Soup

(A Rare Example of a Marriage of Opposites Which Actually Works)

This is peace-making soup because everyone in my family loves it and I make it when I want to tell them that I love them. (What do I make them when I don't love them? Peanut-butter sandwiches, okay? Is that good enough for you?!)

First you must make a chicken stock or the vegetarian equivalent thereof. If you are feeling particularly kind and loving, take some pieces of

chicken and boil them steadfastly with

slices of ginger and a

half an onion. You must then strain the soup, take the meat off the bones, shred it and add it to the soup. (If you don't make the stock from scratch, don't forget to add some grated ginger to your canned broth or bouillon.)

Once you have a delicious stock (about six cups) add:

1 cup cubed tofu

2 tablespoons soy sauce

2 tablespoons lemon juice or vinegar

ground pepper

1/4 teaspoon sugar

Taste and adjust the seasonings to your satisfaction. While that is gently simmering take

1/4 cup water and mix it with

2 tablespoons cornstarch. Pour into the soup to thicken, stirring vigorously.

Then beat

an **egg or two.** When the soup is very hot but not boiling hard, drizzle the egg into the broth in a thin stream. Do not stir immediately, or the egg will thicken the soup in a most unpleasant way instead of floating to the top of the pot in the traditional shred-like pieces.

Serve with sticky white rice, if that's how your partner thinks rice should be. You can make him eat brown rice (for his health, you know) tomorrow.

TWENTY-TWO

They say never take marital advice from someone who is in a relationship you don't admire. I think my mom and dad had a good relationship. As Mom says, they tend to agree more and more the longer Dad has been dead. But according to both my parents' reports (and believe me, when I was a teenager, I asked), it was a good relationship.

"You and Daddy got along," I said plaintively, shortly after I plunked myself on Mom's doorstep. "I thought people are supposed to repeat their parents' patterns! What's wrong with me?"

"Well," said my mother, "I was a lot happier once I accepted the fact that your father was going to work himself to death on the farm, so I might as well go out and get myself a life."

When I got back home, my cousin Shirley offered me another job, a kind of overnight nannying position. I thought about Brian, asked myself what I thought he was going to do for me if I hung around home, and decided I might as well go to work.

"Who knows," I thought. "Maybe things will get better if we're not together all the time." Actually, it was good for us as a couple. Brian got a good sleep once in a while without the kids roaring around; I came home eager to see him again. That part worked out well.

Shirley's job had expanded. She had to start spending half her work week in her parent-company's city. She needed someone to come to her house on Tuesday or Wednesday (it varied), make it feel like a home and prevent her kids and their friends from holding impromptu parties till she came back home at the end of the week. My role was to show up with my kids before Shirley's twelve-year-old got home from school, make supper, clean up, make sure the fifteen-year-old came home, send everyone to bed and get them off to school in the morning. As far as I was concerned, in some ways it was the perfect employment solution. I was making money while I stayed home with my kids. Maybe it wasn't my home we were staying in, but at least it was a home.

Yes, initially it was difficult for all the children to adjust. But I told myself my kids would have had a far more traumatic adjustment to make if I had divorced their father, and felt virtuous. As for Shirley, she allowed herself a little guilt at first (and of course her kids did their best to capitalize on that) but she really didn't have much choice. She either had to accommodate her "changing work place" or take the boot.

Employment in the modern world. So many people are waiting in line for each and every little job, it kinda puts a pin in your butt. "Jump? But of course! I do pole vaulting, standing long jump, spring board, back flips, the limbo, whatever you want!" But you might as well save your breath to busk in the street, because that newspaper advertisement was a formality; the job is already slated for the boss's cousin. Shirley got me every job I've ever had in this town. (Incidentally, when my old filing job came up again, I took that back too.)

Yep, I went to work. It wasn't only that economic independence is always good and spare change comes in handy. It wasn't just that Shirley needed me (because while she could easily have found another nanny for her buck, she would have been hard pressed to find one who loved her kids as much as I did. Or cleaned her bathroom and fridge as tolerantly.) And of course, a job you didn't have to grovel for is a Wonderful Thing.

I took Shirley's job for all those reasons but the big kicker was knock-kneed, basement-bellied, freak-out-and-do-the-funky-chicken *fear* that sent me off to work. Actually, Brian and I were okay for spare change ourselves. Treading water, anyway; losing no ground. But my friends! Oh, my poor friends! They were taking a shit kicking. Except for Shirley, they were all unemployed.

And there was no work. For example, Sarah put in five applications a week for three months and only got three interviews. And she's gorgeous, an absolutely stunningly beautiful blond, which is supposed to be a real asset in the job market. (In fact, I know a woman who actually wore a blond wig until her probation period was over.) Some of my secretarial friends had contract work; a little bit here, a little bit there, but no security. A government town works like that. As well as avoiding the payment of benefits by hiring part-time staff, the government likes contracts because employment statistics can be quickly and easily manipulated depending on whether it's more advantageous to their public image to adjust budget or employment figures.

A few years ago, I used to secretly believe that people who had real jobs (you know, full-time jobs with benefits, making real money) needed to learn to live on less money with fewer benefits so that their jobs could be split in half and more people could be employed. And those hard-working types would get some spare time, which they desperately needed.

I thought that would be a more practical solution to the unemployment crisis than forcing the people with real jobs to accept fewer benefits and pay higher taxes to support all the unemployed masses. However, in a bizarre way, that's what has happened, except that instead of working half days or half weeks, people are working half years, and looking for work the other half. So they're making less money, but they don't get the free time either—a lose/lose situation. While contract work is better than no work at all, it sure plays havoc with the psyche when you don't know whether you'll be employed from month to month. And there still isn't enough work.

On the other hand, what do I know about economics? I don't even listen to the news except when I'm feeling exceptionally stable emotionally. ("Please tell me if anything happens," I said to Brian. "I don't want to look too stupid." I thought he'd like that kind of thing: neutral topics of conversation. He could feel as though he was working at the relationship because he was reporting to me.)

Actually, I do know one thing for sure, and that is that the growing discrepancy between the rich and the poor is not a good thing. Globally or locally.

To illustrate. I was walking through the neighborhood on a beautiful day. This could be the world's nicest neighborhood. Comfortably middle class, maybe even upper middle class, right by the ocean, with sky-high real estate prices even during a recession. I was walking along with the kids, looking at the gardens and worrying about money (like I said, it's a twitch I have) and I saw a piece of garbage on the lawn of a very nice house.

Now, I am a garbage picker by nature. Carry your own, and a little bit more, that's what I figure, because from those to whom much has been given, much is expected, and clearly I've been given much, in my opinion. Anyway, I saw this candy wrapper on the lawn, and I was making a passing swoop to pick it up, you know, without breaking my pace or tripping over the stroller, and I stopped in mid-air and thought, "Why should I pick up garbage for rich people?"

And then I was horrified! What a downright ugly attitude! I thought I understood vandalism for the first time. From my uncharitable thought to actively throwing garbage onto someone's property is not such a very big step. And all it takes is a sense of being hard done by, the supposition that others are better off than you are, the feeling that you don't have a chance, that others have had all the breaks, that there is no place or space for you in the world.

The crazy thing is, the people whose lawn I walked by? I don't know anything about them! It's entirely possible they too feel hard done by, not in control. Pressured by taxes and the high cost of living. Unable to guarantee that their grandchildren or even their children get decent jobs and have a chance at a good life.

Who feels that they have enough? Who feels secure? I'm ashamed when I catch myself jumping to conclusions just because someone drives a nice car or lives in a house instead of an apartment. No one's job is sanctified and some of those seemingly okay people would be toast in a month if the ax came down. We need to stop slagging each other. We are all sinking. To quote Brian, some of us are on the *Titanic* and some are on a slow leaky boat.

That's another thing I know for sure. No one is exempt. Maybe that's an advantage of the economic situation getting as bad as it has. Take the middle-aged business person who pulled himself up by his bootstraps in the 1950s and '60s and retired early with his golden handshake and sits there on his pile saying, "I made it on my own—what's wrong with you, you lazy sod?" There are only a few of those old die-hard types left because everyone knows someone who's drowning—everyone with a shred of sense knows that "there but for the grace of God go I."

By now, almost everyone has peers, children, grandchildren or displaced co-workers who for some reason got ousted, or never had a chance and are sliding down the mountain. Yes, for one brief moment in history there was a generation who retired in their fifties. But it happened on the back and bones of our planet and furthermore, it will never happen again.

And there are a whole bunch of young people out there who can't believe that the game is over before they got their Twinkies. Shirley's kids for example.

Brownies Better Than Twinkies

I've never been able to understand what's so great about Twinkies. Just think, if they last as long on the shelf as their package date says they do, what the heck do they put in that cream filling? There must be enough preservatives in there to mummify your stomach. Okay, so they've got sugar in them. So do these brownies, and you get much more chocolate for your buck.

I swear this is the "basic black" recipe. Brownies are always in fashion; you can dress them up—you can dress them down. You can serve them fresh to unexpected guests in twenty minutes flat, or you can divide the whole pan-full by the number of bodies at the trough and everyone gets his or her chocolate fix for the day, no leftovers. With a little practice and pizzazz, you don't even have to measure.

Turn the oven on to 350°F and grab a saucepan. In it, melt
1/4 cup butter
Add
3/4 cup brown sugar
3 tablespoons cocoa. That should lower the heat enough to add
1 egg. Throw in a
pinch of salt
1/2 cup white flour
1/2 teaspoon baking powder

Stir well, place the batter in a greased pan and set the timer for 15 minutes.

So much for the simple version. And it is perfect. But if you want to mess with perfection, you can try adding
1/2 cup pecans
1/2 cup chocolate chips

This version is also heavenly, but still conservative. So if you want a plate of something a little bit different, but truly scrumptious, add the **zest of one orange** to the batter.

Who needs Twinkies? Pooh! Not me!

TWENTY-THREE

What is wrong with this picture? Here we have a whole lot of boomers with their teenage kids and those kids have every material advantage that can be conceived of—have had since infancy. Our cultural expectation is that these kids will move out when they reach legal age. Or thereabouts. Failure to do so is still a failure. Yet how is this feat of independence to be accomplished in this economic climate, where permanent jobs and benefits are a thing of the past and adults do paper routes to supplement their incomes?

You can't get a job without experience and who's going to give you experience? This is a terrifying prospect for everyone concerned. In addition, the gap between what's available to the home-grown teenager and the young adult out on his or her own is too great. These kids are used to comfort. They want and expect it. Yet they will probably never achieve the level of affluence that their parents did. The planet cannot support it.

Judging only from my experience with Shirley's kids and their friends, this economic reality seemed to sort of sink in some time around the age of fifteen or sixteen, prior to which time I bit my tongue a lot. I wanted to bellow, "You don't know how good you've got it or how soon it's going to end! Say 'Thank you' while you're taking advantage of your mother!"

Clearly I had become the older generation, a process that was amazingly painless, I must say. Arriving at the Uncool. Far out.

However, while I was concerned for my charges' generation and also afraid for our society with this growing base of angry and frustrated youth, I have to confess there was also a big dose of resentment there for me. Some of these kids easily had more disposable income than I did. (Some of them had more disposable income than Shirley, too.) The other thing that they had which I didn't was leisure time. And lots of it. The teenagers I knew appeared to have endless free time. Yet all around me were parents and adults who had none. Why?

The grown-ups (of which I was now obviously one) wore out their Reeboks trying to juggle the demands of family, home maintenance, civic duty and career. If they didn't have a career, they were scrambling to balance their collections of bit jobs, as I was, in an effort to make enough money cumulatively to stay solvent. We battled through our crowding obligations like well-bred waiters at rush hour, managing it all—and at the end of the day, we peed before we sank into bed exhausted, read a self-help book for ten minutes before falling asleep with our mouths open, a little seam of drool from lip to pillow shimmering in the light of the bed lamp we were too tired to turn off. And part of our seemingly endless task list apparently included entertaining those kids, who from their first lisped syllables to their adolescent sulks did not cease with their common mantra: "I'm bored!"

And why do parents take that on? Because they don't want their kids on the streets, that's why. My cousin comes from a family of seven.

"How did your mother cope?" I asked him.

"She turned us out in the morning and she let us back in at night to eat," he said. "The whole block was our back yard. We had any number of mothers."

These days we don't send our kids alone to the park. Whether it is actually more dangerous out there than it used to be, or whether we just perceive that it is does not matter. It isn't done. Kids either have to be supervised or plugged into the TV—which would you choose, day after day after day? And these children turn into teenagers. What kind of adults will this kind of parenting produce? Tell me, what in their experience could possibly prepare them for the fact that, should they make it to adulthood, they will never ever have free time again?

No wonder parents get burned out. Maybe appliances made our grunt work easier but the emotional drain of being on call twenty-four hours a day definitely takes its toll.

Let's face it. We're talking jealousy here. My own teenage years were so painful, so filled with angst, I wouldn't want 'em back. I remember I knew I wanted to be somebody and do something but I didn't know who or what. Yet I recall with longing that time when I lay for hours on my bed just staring endlessly at the ceiling. What a luxury. (I really must indulge that fantasy soon and purge myself of desire before I get my wish and God turns me into a paraplegic with plenty of time to lie there staring at the ceiling again.)

Having got that out of my system, I've got to say I loved Shirley's kids. They were great kids — thoughtful, interesting, fun. Kinda gave a person hope. And they were mine in a way, though I did not feel it was my job to raise them. I felt my first priority was to minimize the amount of disruption in their home life; to make them feel stable and secure. That was the most important thing. So I didn't try to make them clean up as much as I probably ought to have done. I tried to treat them respectfully and encouraged them to help me out of respect, rather than by demand. And I baked a lot.

Finding meals that everyone would eat was certainly a challenge. To begin with, Shirley's kids wouldn't eat leftovers so I tried to make things that Shirley could eat if necessary when she came home. Unfortunately, Shirley was allergic to sulfites and wheat, just for starters. Her daughter didn't like meat or hot spices, Mura ate only carbohydrates, and I am indebted to dinosaurs of the herbivore persuasion for the fact that Hiroshi has tried vegetables at all. Shirley's son ate almost anything and lots of it but he drew the line at tofu. I am a little embarrassed to admit that I made cinnamon buns almost once a week and called them supper. Pizza was also successful and pasta covered for emergencies, although some ate it plain with butter, no sauce.

I became gradually but completely re-enamored of Brian, who likes leftovers and eats almost anything but fish. I came home and made scrumptious dishes like zucchini enchiladas in creamy tomato sauce or my sister's sage meat loaf with baked potatoes or rarebit with sherried mushrooms on whole-wheat bread. Maybe it was a strange way to fall back in love, but I'll take my paradise where I find it, thank you very much.

I was always glad to get back to my own home—my own mess, grubby marks made by my own grubby fingers, my own dust bunnies. My own coffee beans in the freezer, my own condiments, and the certain knowledge that if I wanted to bake a cake, there were poppy seeds in the cupboard, sweet butter in the freezer and lemons in the fridge.

But it was good. I felt good. At that stage of my life, there were safety pins everywhere, my personal rabbit's foot, symbolic guarantee that given almost any emergency, I would be able to hold it together, keep the shit in. Money was good. Money is "only money" when you have some, but when you don't, it is a hugely stressful fight for survival. I had some; it was nice.

Hiroshi was growing up, getting sophisticated. "You ask my mother," I overhead him say. "If I ask her she'll say 'No.' " Mura turned one. That girl definitely had the power! Total body satisfaction. She was solid, determined, dispassionately affectionate and happy. Hiroshi zinged. Mura hummed.

Shirley's daughter did her homework while I put my kids to sleep and then sat around and chatted until I sent her off to bed. Her brother grew another eight inches, got his braces off, and honed his debating skills for my admiring entertainment. I had two homes, two families, two lives, two jobs, and not a minute to spare.

"*Roses are red, as everyone knows,*" I wrote on Shirley's Valentine card, "*We should have got married a long time ago.*" Everybody ought to have a wife.

Shirley's kids weren't really my kids and the real proof of that was how incredibly well-behaved they were for me. They caused me so little grief. They saved it up for Shirley when she came home. Having been well brought up, they knew how to behave toward outsiders. As I was not their mother they did not feel compelled to rebel against me.

Shirley and I figured we'd accidentally stumbled on the perfect way to raise teenagers. She got a rejuvenating break, came home feeling loving and eager to see her offspring, ready for the battle, and her kids learned to be electronically connected. As long as Shirley wore her pager, she was available any time. Her kids got time out from the hard job of gently breaking away from the nest, little cousins to play with, occasional baby-sitting commissions, another interested adult in their lives and as many cinnamon buns as they could scarf down. I got cash in my hand, the pleasure of knowing and loving Shirley's kids and their friends and a sneak preview of what might be in store for me in the parenting department.

So did my work experience change the way I parented my own children? Yes, I'd have to say it did. Having teenagers and their friends hanging about sharply reminded me to treat my own kids with respect. Consistently. Because I want to be treated with respect. Having those hulking headbangers slamming around the kitchen was a pretty good reminder. They're so big! But Hiro and Mura were small.

"I know how I want you to speak to me when you're bigger. I'll show you how it is done. How 'bout we start right now. While you're much smaller than I am . . ." Mind you, I also learned this: never judge someone else's parenting results. Try to do better, yes, but never judge. Never say, "I won't let my kid lip me like that. I won't tolerate that kind of behavior." That's like saying you won't let your baby cry on the airplane. That's asking for an illustration of the glass-house principle. God'll get you for that one!

Cinnamon Buns (and Potato Filling)

Any standard bread dough will do. This is the one I use:
Proof:
1 tablespoon yeast
1 tablespoon sugar
1/2 cup warm water

While you're waiting for that to bubble, mix:
1 egg
2 cups warm water
1/2 cup oil
1/2 teaspoon salt
1/4 cup sugar
4 cups flour
1/2 teaspoon powdered ginger
2 tablespoons lemon juice

Add the yeast mixture to the dough. You can now take a ten-minute break if you wish or you can carry on adding
flour until the bread is the right consistency (**about 4 more cups**).
All the usual rules apply. Knead it long enough, think happy thoughts while you're punching, keep out of drafts. You can use all white flour or a combination of white and brown or all brown if you're confident.

Let the dough rise to double, punch it down and divide it into two. Roll it into a square. Get your pans out (use something with a good lip so you don't get sugar all over the oven). Take out the
sugar
butter and
cinnamon (and **nutmeg and cloves** if you like to mess with tradition).

When everything is ready, dip your paws in the butter, grease the pans and slather the dough. Sprinkle liberally with brown sugar and spices. Roll up the dough into a log and cut into slices. Put them in the pan. I like mine crammed close together so that they rise up instead of across. Let them rise to double while you pre-heat the oven to 350°F. Bake till golden brown. Turn them out of the pan when they're done, before the sugar hardens into cement.

Now, considering this is supper, you might like to fill the second half of the dough with something more substantial. Take
two strips of bacon, mince them and fry to almost crisp. You can omit this step and use
olive oil if you prefer. Then gently sauté
chopped onions
crushed garlic and maybe some
finely chopped carrots and
celery. While that is cooking, peel and chop
potatoes into tiny cubes. Sauté them as well. Season with
salt, pepper, basil, oregano, marjoram, or **thyme** in any combination.
Grated cheese and
black olives are also nice.

When the filling is ready, take a golf-ball sized whack of dough and roll it into a circle about 1/4 inch thick. Put as much filling in as you can, fold the circle in half and crimp the edges.
Brush with
milk or
egg if you want to be fancy. Bake till golden brown.

TWENTY-FOUR

Yes, my employment situation was pretty good. However, don't you find it a diversion to consider the things that are left unsaid? For example, I just described a job that I took and worked at for almost a year and a half, and I've chatted you up to a kind of natural stopping place. I've pretty much told the truth to the best of my abilities, in a general way. But of course, one can't tell everything.

So I didn't even mention Shirley's oldest son, her seventeen-year-old, who moved in with his dad half way through my term of employment, and all the upheaval that occurred in Shirley's life because of it. He was never "my" boy; he was too old for a nanny in the first place and he was seldom home anyway. I liked him and love him still without having a single common point of juncture with him other than family. But for the purposes of this story, it's easier just to omit him. Pretend he never even existed.

Well and good, as an example. So what else hasn't been said? I leave it for you to conjecture. Meanwhile, as I was living through that stretch of a year and a half which I described just moments ago as "pretty good," I had, during the same time period, a year of disasters. Yes, while I was cheerfully (or not) carrying on, presenting homemade meals night after night in one or the other of my two homes and taking the bus back and forth with my entourage, I also had the Year From Hell. I felt like I had a membership in the "Crisis of the Month" club.

It started in November. I was in a sort of emotional backwater. A nice quiet space. I was feeling good. Everything pretty well under control. One night after the kids were in bed, I was hanging out of my window smoking the last cigarette in my pack. I thought to myself, as I often did, "What if this was the last cigarette I ever smoked? Wouldn't that be something? I should try and quit again. This is probably a good time to try to quit smoking." I fully intended to go out and buy another package of cigarettes the following afternoon. I felt lazy. Cat lazy, stretching out the window, blowing smoke into the night sky. "Send me a dream to help me quit smoking," I told the moon, laughing. Then I went to bed.

And I had one of the realest dreams I have ever had. Technicolor. Big screen. I had the principal part. I dreamed I wasn't feeling well. I hate doctors. But I wasn't feeling well for a long time so eventually I went to the doctor. The doctor sent me to the specialist and I had a whole battery of tests, and that's always pleasant, but what was even lovelier still was—I had cancer. I had cancer, it was really bad, and I had a whole lot of chemotherapy I didn't really want to have but I couldn't live without. I had a smorgasbord, a whole assortment. It was awful. But I went into remission. I had a couple of years. And then it came back. I was dying. I had an eight-year-old boy, and a five-year-old daughter, and I was going to leave them. And in my dream, there was nothing I could do about it.

I remember that as a very young child (definitely preschool, but I'm not sure how old), I lay on the floor pushing a heavy door with my foot, thinking, "If it closes there is a God; if it swings back there is no God." For as long as I can remember, I have always been fascinated with death. In grade six while everyone else was doing their book reports on their favorite rock stars' autobiographies, I was consumed by *On Death and Dying* by Elizabeth Kubler-Ross. Oh, the time I've spent wondering about God and death. Especially together. Is there an afterlife? What happens then? How does it feel to die? Wouldn't it be good to *know*? I have always hoped to live so fully, so beautifully that I could die without regrets. I wanted to leave the doorway of my life with enthusiasm, eager to undertake life's last and greatest adventure.

It was two weeks *after* my dream that I even noticed how that level of interest was lacking on my own (dream-state) deathbed. Where was all my philosophy, my curiosity, my religion? Not a flicker of a thought did I spare in that direction! For once my feelings were pure and unadulterated. In my dream, I did not want to die. I did not want to leave my children. I know how devastating it is to have a parent go away. At least my father had had the decency to wait until I was eighteen before he had his accident.

I woke up with a start clutching at my babies on either side of me, frantically patting the mounds of bedding, making sure they were there. It took me a moment to realize it was just a dream: I wasn't dead, looking down on them, blessing them from above, a ghost of a mother. I sank back into my pillows, awash with gratitude. For whatever reason, it seemed I had been given a second chance.

★★★★★

That was November. The first few weeks without cigarettes are always—what can one say? They are simply horrid, and that's all there is to it. Maybe persons of greater character than myself are able to enjoy themselves, but not I, not any of the twenty or so times I've been through "the first weeks." But I persevered. I believed that if I had so much as one puff my dream would lose all its magical power and I would go spiraling down into the well of my addiction. So I sweated through my initiation period the usual way except that I was motivated as never before. And I did not smoke.

If you are the kind of person (and I know I am) who tends to commit herself to too many projects and gets about half way through before noticing not only are you not having fun any more, but there are deep black circles under your eyes, your hands are shaking, and your family has gone from hysterical to apathetic-bordering-on-comatose (but you have to keep going because you *promised*), then Christmas can be the most disastrous season of the year.

In December, I did the jerky turkey thing: I spread myself out on a platter and carved myself up. I don't know, maybe my decision-making processes were having a nic-fit or something but at any rate I truly over did it. I made wrapping paper and origami boxes and candy and trays of goodies for my neighbors and the staff at Brian's favorite video store, little chocolate-dipped peanut-butter Rice Krispies balls for heaven's sake! I made presents and bought presents and painted a Christmas tree on a huge piece of paper on our tack board. Hiroshi festooned it with our decorations hung by pins.

To top it all off, I made little Playdough cutouts, which had to dry and then we painted and we decorated them and then we shellacked them, and each of these steps had to be done twice, once on each side. "Jo," I said, "are you out of your mind? Are you crazy? Would you please stop!" Then I shellacked one more time because once you've come that far, you might as well do it right. December 25th finally came around like a steamroller and I just kind of lay there, flat-like, saying, "What happened? Where am I?"

But I didn't smoke.

January arrived and for once I didn't have to quit smoking, so I had a private little celebration all my own. I ate, of course: adult cookies, infused with coffee, studded with cashews and chocolate chips and glazed with rum and icing sugar.

A couple of days later I was at the playground with my friend, Jen. She had a son Mura's age and she worked four days a week. She said she was stuck for a sitter for Wednesday and I said if the worst came to the worst I'd take Marlo for her. The worst did come to the worst—and then I made it worse yet. I was getting ready to take all three kids for an outing. Jen's house has a little postage-stamp porch. On one side there is a screen door and some very steep stairs. On the other side there is a very heavy door. We were all in the porch. Leaving is always terrible, as any parent will tell you, so my mind was ticking away: "Got the stroller, got the snacks, got the shoes on, got the kids."

"Hiroshi," I said sharply, "please shut that screen door; I'm afraid Marlo will fall down those stairs," and while I said it, I shut the heavy door. I had time to think, "Gee this door is sticky," and *crunch*. That was Marlo's finger.

I thought I'd taken it off. Back into the house, apply pressure, dial 911, look for a clean cloth, apply pressure. Mura was on my back in the pack, Hiroshi was having hysterics. I shut him up in the bedroom. Both babies were wailing. Apply pressure. Wait for the ambulance. The finger seemed to be in one piece but I couldn't tell how bad the damage was or if it would fall off. I couldn't keep Marlo stable and immobile and look for ice at the same time. There was blood all over. Apply pressure. Wait for the ambulance.

So the ambulance came and took Marlo away. The driver called Jen and told her to meet him at the hospital. I sent Marlo's favorite stuffed toy. And suddenly there was this big quiet in the house. Hiroshi peeked his head out from the bedroom. I began to clean up the blood.

From point A to point B. You see, at the time I had no way of knowing how it was all going to end. Jen is a very practical, strong person. "If this is the worst that ever happens to him, he'll be lucky," she said when she called from the hospital. Of course that was true; it was not the end of the world, but can you imagine how I felt? I had damaged her perfect, so perfect boy! Born with all his fingers and toes—and I took one off. Oh, it was terrible. I felt like a criminal. I kept thinking, "If this is how you feel when you hurt someone's baby, how would you feel if you were in a car accident and you killed someone?"

Marlo had reconstructive surgery. The finger was not completely detached; in fact, I just missed the bone by a hair. A year later, you had to look closely to see his scars.

"Jen," said Hiroshi the next time we saw her, "it wasn't actually me who did that."

I didn't smoke.

Scones Lighter Than Air

(To Soothe a Heavy Heart)

This recipe has almost all of my favorite qualities. It's fast, it's forgiving and it's comforting food.

Set the oven to 400°F. Yes, 400°F. Scones need a good hot oven to rise properly. Haul out a cookie sheet.

In a big bowl, grate
1 cup sharp cheese. Cheddar is good. Gouda is good. Havarti is not so good.
Combine with:
1 cup each white and **brown flour**
1 tablespoon baking powder
1/4 teaspoon salt
1 teaspoon dry mustard

Now you want to add
1/4 cup butter. I like to keep an extra butter in the freezer, and my favorite trick is to pull that out and grate approximately 1/4 cup into the flour. But if you don't want to do that, just remember, what you're aiming for is butter than hasn't melted into the flour because you'll lose the flaky effect if the butter is too soft. So don't handle the butter too much or use warm butter, or worse yet, melted butter.
Make a well in your buttery flour. Pour in
1 large beaten egg and
1/2 to 3/4 cup milk

Now, you want to combine the ingredients, and then gently knead the dough into a ball. Pat it down into a circle, place it on the cookie sheet, cut into eighths like a pie, and separate the pieces slightly. Sprinkle some cheese over the tops if you like.

Bake for just over 15 minutes. Just a wee tad over. You're aiming for golden brown but not the least bit burned.

Eat slathered with butter.

TWENTY-FIVE

In February Mom came out for her annual month at her favorite beachside bed and breakfast. She did some looking around for a couple of weeks and then she said, "Let's buy a condo!" Yeeeah, right, Mom, let's fly to the moon. Let's pick a bale of cotton. Let's get naked and dance the Charleston down Main Street.

"No, no," she said, "I'm serious. We can do this. I'll make the down payment, and you and Brian can handle the mortgage. You have to pay rent one way or another; what's the difference?"

I suppose I should take responsibility for starting that ball rolling, because I was the one who kept talking about finding a bigger place. I loved our apartment, with its big kitchen looking out over a huge weeping willow. While I cooked, the children raced cars on the crumbling squares of ancient linoleum, or painted lavishly colorful masterpieces, seated at the plank which was our table. True, the bathroom was tiny (just a toilet, basin and bath, and holding a baby, I could barely turn around in it without scraping an elbow), but the living room was large and the light was good.

But although our apartment had seemed so vast and luxurious when we moved in, our family had grown. The biggest problem was that Brian couldn't sleep. The kitchen and the only bedroom were directly adjacent to each other. I did dishes right by Brian's left ear. I felt remorse every time he stumbled out to pee.

And, the building was getting old, just waiting to become more valuable as land than as rental property. The inside needed a paint job desperately. The red carpets were threadbare.

"Let's face it, it's a dump," Mom said. Ouch!

Why, you might ask, would one hesitate, if one had a parent willing to plunk a down payment onto a property that one would subsequently own? Why would one question such a gift? Well, perhaps one would like to accomplish something for oneself for a change, eh? Perhaps one might think, "Here I am, in the middle of my life, and my mother is *still* bailing me out. When will I ever be independent? When will I be strong and self sufficient?"

"Plenty of very successful people have had help from their parents," my mother chided.

That's not all. Real estate on the west coast is exorbitantly high. Let's face it—Vancouver Island is Canada's Hawaii. Same volcano chain. Okay, we're a little farther north but we've still got the best climate in the country. It snows maybe once a year, just to make us feel like real Canadians but the crocuses start coming out in February. Consequently, what would buy a very fine house on the prairies won't buy a bachelor suite in a bad neighborhood here.

"What if real estate crashes and we can't get your investment money back?" I said to my mother.

"I'll take that chance," she replied.

That's not all. While Brian had been cheerfully (or not) paying bills for years and years as a bartender, the night club he worked for routinely threatened to disband. Fear of unemployment was just a constant in our lives. What if Brian lost his job?

"You will still have to live somewhere," my mother said. "If Brian loses his job, he will find another one. If that doesn't happen right away, I'll help you for a while. If you need to move, we'll find a tenant, or I'll come out and live here for a bit. We can always sell. If Armageddon arrives, my investment will be the least of our worries. I just hate to see you throw your money away in rent."

"I'm afraid of losing your money," I said. "I'm so talented that way."

Mom said, "I guess I'll put my money where I want to. Look, every time I go to invest in something that looks profitable it turns out to be a company which exploits workers in Taiwan or uses DDT in Poland. Let's buy a condo. When I'm old I'll come out and live with you over the winter, and you can take care of me."

All that anxiety and we hadn't even started. Then we called up my friend the real estate agent and made a list of everything we wanted.

Then there was the financial thing. The bank didn't want us, but the mortgage brokers were happy to help us spend more than we should have. Then there were schedules to align and baby-sitters to get while we drove around looking at places. Nothing affordable seemed suitable. Finally, we found an apartment that made my skin crinkle from the moment we first drove up.

"This is it," I said to myself. Two bedrooms, in our own neighborhood, close to a good school, fifteen minutes walk from downtown, ten minutes walk to the sea. The building was in good condition, the suite in question immaculate. In the spacious living room, big french windows faced north, looking over assorted trees. All four of us could get into the bathroom at the same time, and there was a big counter— imagine! *And* there was a tiny second bathroom off a huge walk-in closet (future private space for a teenager?) in the master bedroom.

It was the only condo listed in our neighborhood which didn't have a regulation prohibiting children. We talked to the woman who rented the suite we wanted to buy. "Are there any kids in the building?" we asked.

"Oh yes, there is a two-year-old downstairs, and an eleven-year-old right next door. I never hear them." Wonderful!

So then there was the deciding and then there was telling Brian we'd planned how to spend his pay cheques for the next twenty years, and then we had to take him around to see the apartment. Some people love driving around, poking into places to see what they are like inside. Brian would be the polar opposite of that person. He was ready to buy sight unseen as long as he didn't have to shop. Then there was making an offer and waiting for a response. And *all of it* was very stressful.

Our offer was accepted so we went and paid for the title search and we dropped the papers off for the lawyer. When we returned to sign up in his office, he said, "There is a by-law stating that no children are allowed without prior approval from the strata council." As it turned out, all the children in the building were in rental units.

I guess we could have turned back right there, but by this time I wasn't willing to give up. I made a billion phone calls and ended up having a meeting with the strata council and off I went with a little prepared speech, letters of recommendation from my neighbors in my old apartment building, cute pictures of my children, and the promise that I would be the kind of neighbor anyone would want to have. Last but not least, I brought a huge platter of freshly baked cookies, two kinds, still smelling strongly of applesauce and cinnamon, and mint extract and chocolate. I bribed them with baking. And the council hemmed and hawed, and finally they gave me permission to purchase.

Then March came and there was more lawyer stuff to do and more mortgage stuff and faxes and appointments and more baby-sitters. It makes me tired just to write about it. I worried intensely about moving into a place potentially hostile toward children, especially since there was no reverse mode. Then there was packing and cleaning and April came and we took possession over the Easter weekend. I had my friends all lined up to help me paint the cupboards which were very dark brown and unbearable. I don't know who invented the galley kitchen but in my dreams, I would have my kitchen, dining room and living room all in one, with windows on three sides. However, the condo kitchen was much brighter after we whited out the cupboards.

And then we moved. Brian coerced his workmates into showing up on a Sunday afternoon, loading everything we owned onto the back of a truck and unceremoniously dumping it in our new living room. We slept on the floor surrounded by ominous boxes, like camping in the shadows of the walls of a fortress. Hiro's favorite stuffed whale went missing, Brian couldn't find his toothbrush and Mura screamed in sympathy. Just your average moving mess.

And then I went to work. I don't mean unpacking and sorting and arranging and all of those slogging chores, though I did those too. I went to work to woo my neighbors. I had my campaign all planned out, but I had no idea how incredibly stressful I would find it. I was used to being loved. My old neighbors wept to see us go. Now I had a whole new set of conquests to make and if I failed, there was no escape.

So I stood on my head. It was no problem to be friendly—my father does that for me: I just sit back and watch his genes take control of my body. I jumped through smaller hoops than that though. I dropped notes off to my closest neighbors, greeting them and asking them to give us a call if they found we were too noisy. I especially solicited Anne, the woman below us, because she was the person most directly affected by our presence. Sad but true, when the gentle lady above us trod softly across the floor in her stocking feet, we heard her. I could, therefore, just imagine how Mura and Hiro sounded elephanting across the living room. Anne told me they made her chandelier swing.

However, the main problem was that Mura woke up crying in the night. We compromised. Anne put in earplugs. We moved our family bed into the living room, as far away from where Anne slept as possible, right next to the corner of the building. After work, Brian liked to unwind by watching TV, so I put that in the middle room where he could relax without waking us up. I put a bed in the back room so that when the kids woke up in the morning, Brian could heave himself upright, stumble down the hallway, close the door and fall into bed alone to finish his sleep. Essentially, the kids and I lived in one room.

I had Anne up for coffee, because one feels significantly different about the children one knows than "those spoiled brats upstairs." I fed her brownies, and German cookies with lemon peel, honey and almonds. I invited her to the kids' birthday parties; she wisely passed on that and came up for leftover cheesecake afterwards, but at least she knew when to take her walk on those occasions.

Fortunately Anne was easy to love, but it took us quite a while to be pleased about being neighbors. I wasn't very happy for the whole month of May. But I didn't smoke.

Birthday/Bribe Cheesecake

Cheesecake is a lovely thing. It is dead easy to make, it's elegant and impressive, and you're supposed to make it ahead so you can get it over with. Okay, it's expensive, but here's a helpful little fact: Frozen cream cheese works just fine; you can buy it on sale and hoard it. Those big, solid chocolate rabbits which are incredibly cheap just after Easter freeze well too. A word of warning on the bunnies though: they're sweeter than regular baking chocolate, so cut back on the sugar in the cheesecake. Here goes!

Preheat the oven to 375°F.
Press
1 cup wafers (chocolate or **graham)** and
1/4 cup melted butter into a spring-form pan. You can use
coconut, lemon zest or chopped nuts in the crust too, depending on your passion.

Then blend
3 (250 g.) packages softened cream cheese. When that's good and soft, add
3 eggs one at a time, and then
3/4 cup sugar.

Now add flavoring.
Vanilla, melted chocolate or **almond extract** are all nice choices. If you want to be fancy, you can divide the batter in two and make a two-layer cheesecake, say, bottom half chocolate and top half vanilla. Pour the batter over the crumbs.

Bake at 375°F for 45 minutes.

If you want to, cool the cake out for 30 minutes, and glaze it with
1 cup of sour cream mixed with
2 tablespoons sugar or **2 squares melted chocolate** and bake exactly ten more minutes.

Now chill the cake until you want to use it. If you heartily wish to impress yourself and your guests, also make a fruit sauce and chill that. Take, for example,
frozen strawberries. Boil them, purée them and add

sugar to taste. When you present your cheesecake, ladle this sauce over it. Then melt
1 square chocolate with
1 teaspoon vegetable oil. Stir until smooth. Spoon into a little plastic wrap sack. Prick the sack with a toothpick. Now you can gently squeeze chocolate drizzle from the sack over your cheesecake and strawberry sauce. Place a dollop of
whipped cream on top.

Sell to the highest bidder.

TWENTY-SIX

On the last day of May something happened which drove every other problem from my mind entirely, something which occupied me totally for a month.

I came home from the office on a Tuesday, very tired. We did supper (chicken mole in the microwave), baths, stories, the whole routine. Hiroshi went to bed with his daddy. I put Mura into her crib. I took a pot of boiling chicken stock off the stove and put it on the balcony to cool down a bit. It was a warm night, so I didn't close the door. And Mura, who was one and a half and getting more agile by the minute, climbed out of bed, brushed past the curtains, grabbed the handles of the stock pot and sloshed herself with scalding chicken fat. It ran all around the top of her diaper and splashed on her legs. I will never forget her screams.

I do not panic in emergencies, apparently. I had Mura out of her pajamas and into a tub of cold water before I knew what I was doing. I had no idea how much damage had been done, but I bellowed for Brian to call 911. Skin was peeling off in sheets.

The ambulance attendants were calm and efficient. I was still in function/crisis mode. While they poured sterile solution over my shrieking child, I got out of my wet clothes (I'd been in the tub with Mura, holding her down), grabbed my wallet, answered questions for the forms, and remembered to bring quarters for the phone. Then we drove away in the ambulance. (Whenever I hear that siren, my stomach starts to quiver like aspic.)

We didn't wait in Emergency. Doctors were already working on Mura before I finished filling out her forms. I had time to call Shirley, begging her to come right away. Then a nurse came to take me to Mura. She was in a small, bright room full of people in full-length sterile gowns, masks and gloves. The lights—that was what made an impression; that was the moment the knowledge began to penetrate: *This is serious! This is dangerous!*

Someone helped me gown up. Mura's veins were constricted, so the nurses were having trouble getting a needle in to give her morphine and to hook up her I.V. I pressed my face next to her cheek, that soft, curving blossom. Sang in her ear. Held her hand tightly. Promised she would be all right. Brian came in, suited up, stood near me. Shirley had brought him, and Hiroshi.

"Forgive me!" I sobbed.

Poor Bri—who couldn't even bear to hear Hiroshi cry as a baby, watching Mura twist in agony. "Don't blame yourself; don't blame yourself." For his absolution, I will forever be grateful.

Finally they got Mura drugged up. The plastic surgeon came and gave his verdict. There were a couple of places that might need surgical repair, but most of her burns were second degree. The real problem was the percentage of skin which had been damaged. Of course. I hadn't thought of that, but of course: skin is an organ. A decision was made to transfer Mura to the Pediatric Intensive Care Unit instead of keeping her on the Burn Ward in town. I got on the stretcher. They placed my bundled baby in my arms. We wheeled away.

"Goodbye Hiroshi. Mama will be sleeping with Mura tonight. You be a good boy for Daddy." Wave, wave. Into the ambulance. Into the night.

*****

While we were in the emergency room, the plastic surgeon told us we would be looking at two weeks in the hospital. I considered this as we rode in the ambulance. The attendant was very kind. He let me babble, over and over again, how very sorry I was. "And you probably always will be," he said. "But don't forget that's why we call them accidents. You didn't do it intentionally." I felt like I had. I felt like I'd lost all credibility as a mother entirely. I felt like I'd let Mura down. Seeing her in such pain—oh, have mercy.

I told the ambulance attendant, "I always pray to be given my lessons gently. This is too hard," but hardly were the words out of my mouth than I thought, "Bite your tongue! It could have been worse, way, way worse. Maybe this *is* the gentle version of this lesson." But that's supposing life has a reason and a purpose. Otherwise, omit all.

Thank you, thank you. Thank you, God. Thank you, ambulance drivers. Thank you, emerg staff. Thank you, nurses. Thank you, doctors. Thank you, Shirley. Thank you, Brian. Thank God for Universal Health Care. *This is my chant, my spell against evil. Please let it work.*

The Intensive Care staff were a credit to humanity. The nurse who admitted Mura was so capable, so true. Mura had entered narcotic happy-land by this time. The nurse told me that the plan was to keep her stoned through the worst of the pain. They put her in the isolation room. There was a lot of activity, getting her bandaged, hooked up to the drip, monitors fixed on her chest and another on her toe. We'd been so lucky. Her hands were spared, her upper body, her face. She hadn't splashed a single joint, by some stroke of luck.

"Is she all right then? Why does she need all these monitors?"

"Her fluids will be moving around quite a bit," the nurse explained. "She's on a lot of drugs and with so much flesh exposed, there's a serious danger of infection."

That was enough for me! I have never felt so sad, so bad, so scared. Not even when my father died. Because he was dead. Nothing worse could happen. But this! My baby might not be okay. Why, oh why, didn't I shut that door?

I've never written about how much I love her. Things are so different with your second child. You've already begun to take that miraculous love for granted. And Mura was so different from Hiroshi—so different from me. She was direct, opinionated, independent, full of energy to prove any point. Did I say how much I admired her? Wondered at her stubborn power? Did I say that her chubby arms around my neck filled me with gratitude for her very presence? I believed she came from the angels, that they sent her to me, this woman-child I had longed for so much. Oh, my baby.

★★★★★

Finally, all was quiet. There was a room for parents to sleep in, but I could not leave Mura. I was afraid she would leave me. "Bleep, bleep," went the machine, casting an orange glow over everything. I sat in the rocking chair and watched the room fill up with spirits. "Now I lay me down to sleep; nineteen angels round me keep . . ." They were golden, dressed in flowing white, trimmed with midnight blue. Then came the grandmothers, all races of grandmothers, wrinkled and cackling, their swaddling wraps flapping black and dark purple, some with rosaries, some with ropes of the blue and red beads the white man used to buy them off. Then Jesus, white and still as liquid marble, took his place at the foot of the crib, his beautiful lean hands stretched out in benediction. Just as my father and Aunt Jean were arriving, arm in arm, I fell asleep, totally exhausted.

★★★★★

What followed was an emotional marathon. Brian's parents had to be called; they came over on the ferry that same morning. Shirley phoned my mother after dropping Hiroshi and Brian off at our apartment. Mom started driving the next morning. She had farther to go but her presence spared me the anguish of worrying about who was going to look after my son while I stayed in the hospital and Brian worked.

That blessing, for which I was profoundly grateful, made my life very odd! After so much stress and after years of continual juggling to cope with all the facets and demands of my life, being in the hospital was bizarrely restful. I only had one thing to worry about. Suddenly I had enormous, terrible focus. One night, while I was waiting for Mura's bandage change to be completed, I listened to the night nurse list off all the things she had to do in preparation for a weekend trip.

"Well," I said, "two days ago I had a lot of things to do too." I was completely suspended in time.

Part of what got me through was that I wanted to do whatever I could for Mura. I believed that if I fussed and panicked, I would harm her. I thought the more normal and cheerful and calm I could appear, the more relaxed she would be. And why shouldn't that be so? I'd long since observed that children pick up their parents' emotions and amplify them on a daily basis. No one any longer doubts the importance of attitude to disease and recovery. How necessary for me then, at that crucial moment, to choose an emotional stance conducive to Mura's healing.

Gidget goes to the hospital.

Mura slept fitfully all Wednesday. Her face was red from tossing against her flannelette sheets, bloated and puffy from drugs. She already had a routine: dressing changes twice a day. She was bathed and débrided (removal of the dead skin to prevent infection). Medicated dressings were applied and the gauze rewound, returning Mura to her mummy state. The whole bandage was held together by tubular stretch netting. Then I came in with my sterile gown and held her, big bundle, tubes and monitors trailing off behind us. Rock, rock. People came and went. Brian. My in-laws. Shirley. They brought food. During the next week, all my friends came and they all brought food, the sweethearts.

"That's what you always do for us," Jen said, "so we thought that's what you'd want us to do for you."

And Katherine, bless her, came in to give Mura therapeutic touch treatments and color therapy.

Brian brought me a bag of necessities. I was surprised into tears by his thoughtfulness. He remembered to include antacid, because sometimes my stomach hurts when I'm under pressure. But what really impressed me was his choice of books: *Pride and Prejudice* and *Care for the Soul*. He picked out what I wanted so accurately that I thought, "Maybe he *has* been paying attention."

And so it went. After the first night, I couldn't sleep. Thursday my mother came. Mura was still very drugged. *Change her diaper, sing her lullabies, rock, rock. Watch her sleep, soothe her when she wakes. Rock, rock. Try to eat. Try to take a walk. Make some phone calls. Back again. Rock, rock.* I felt anxious if I was away from her for more than a few minutes.

Friday Mura was restless and upset. The nurses and her doctor were playing with her medication, trying to get it right. I spent most of the morning settling my girl, soothing her. When she finally went to sleep, I was exhausted. The nurses encouraged me to take a break. I ate. I was just about to lie down to try to sleep when I heard an announcement over the intercom. "C.A., P.I.C.U." I thought it meant there was a serious emergency incoming to the Pediatric Intensive Care Unit. I thought, "The nurses will be busy. I'll just go down and sit with Mura in case they don't have time to watch her closely."

People were running past me down the corridor. "This is just like TV," I thought. And then I turned the corner and the door of the isolation room, *Mura's room!*, was flung open wide and half the hospital was spilling out, spilling out without gowns on, doctors, nurses, interns, administrators. "Oh my God, oh my God. She's dead. Oh no. Please don't make me do this. I never thought I'd have to do this."

You see, even at that moment, I remembered, you survive. The one you love best in the whole world can die, and you will not. You will carry on. And you will work like a slave to get over the pain. Oh, there can be gifts: increased understanding, empathy, compassion. Eventually. But you will pay dearly for those gifts, for years and years and years.

I didn't feel badly for Mura at that moment. In fact, I could see how it would be very attractive to just float into the arms of all those angels and grandmothers and loving relatives. I felt badly for me. I didn't want to have to live without her; I didn't want to have to climb that mountain.

And I completely fell apart. I left the planet. I watched from above while someone said, "Is this the mum?" and led me away and held my hand and passed me tissues and explained that Mura was okay, she was okay, she just forgot to breathe for a minute; sometimes that happens when you have a lot of drugs on board. Then I heard Mura start to wail and the woman holding my hand told me that was a good sign, and I wept and laughed and wept and finally I crawled back into my body, but it didn't feel like a very safe place to be.

Then the pediatrician came and told me why that wasn't going to happen again and I looked at him and said, "I understand, but it doesn't take a pot of soup to kill a baby. God can take her away from me just any old time for no reason at all."

And then function mode kicked in, and I went into the room and they handed me Mura and I rocked her and settled her and sang her lullabies. She finally went to sleep, but I didn't. When Katherine came in to work her healing magic at that serendipitous moment, I was so grateful to see her that I could have kissed her shoes.

★★★★★

That was Friday. Saturday Mura started to perk up and act merely socially stoned. The nurses wanted to take her off the drip, so I was trying to convince her to consume protein drink. Mura was as malleable as usual: she wanted to make bubbles. She sat on my knee, puffy-faced and inebriated, and received visitors off and on all afternoon. I began to relax.

As the afternoon wore away and our company finally went home, the atmosphere in the unit changed. Where all had been peaceful, suddenly there was an electric hum. At first I didn't trust my feelings, but finally I asked my nurse what was going on.

"Incoming," was all the information she was able to give me. "Close your curtain. We'll keep an eye on the monitor. You don't want to see this."

With the curtains closed in the isolation room the nurses could not actually see Mura through their observation window but by this time, I knew which monitors were supposed to hook up where and a duplicate of Mura's screen bleeped away in the main unit. I sat in my rocking chair and averted my eyes. I felt fragile, like meringue wafers, the kind that just melt away on your tongue.

I needed to know what disaster had occurred—did someone come into McDonald's and take random pot shots at a peewee baseball team? Was someone abused? Because of patient confidentiality, no one could tell me, so I didn't ask. Instead I phoned Shirley, who had connections everywhere. She had just been visiting us; she knew everyone in the respiratory department.

"It's a head injury," Shirley told me. "A girl fell off her bike. The prognosis isn't good." That was all I needed to know.

I went back to Mura's room and sat there and prayed for whoever it was lying there in the next room and for her mother and her daddy and everyone else who cared. I sat there weeping and the hours ticked by and finally the nurse came in and apologized for missing Mura's dressing change so I said that was okay. When she drew back the curtain, the main unit of the P.I.C.U. was empty.

I didn't sleep that night either. Monday morning I cut out the article in the newspaper. She was fifteen. She wasn't wearing a helmet. The reporter quoted the mother, "She was just going to whip over and get some special kind of shampoo, and she's dead. It's unbelievable."

Climbing up the mountain. People do.

★★★★★

After that incident, I lightened up considerably. My girl was going to get better. Okay, she might have a few scars, but it would be something for us to fight about when she became a teenager. With my new-found concentration, I attended to the minute details of Mura's progress. I had to remind myself that I used to have another life, one I had been very involved in. How quickly it faded into insignificance. How questionable was its reality. Maybe I was not really a mother but rather a scientist working on Mars. Possibly any minute I'd wake up and remember I had dreamed I had a baby and spent a week in the P.I.C.U. "Man, what a weird dream I had last night, guys. Musta been something I ate from those astro-tubes."

I learned more about being in the hospital than I had ever wanted to know. When Mura got out of intensive care, we spent another week on the ward before we went home. I was surprised to find that I was afraid to leave. Mura still had open wounds. I was afraid of doing her dressings at home, even with the help of the community nurse. I was afraid I wouldn't be able to give Mura her medications properly. She was very resistant to taking her meds. I was afraid we wouldn't be able to afford her drugs and dressings, which were provided by the hospital as long as Mura was actually on the ward but became my responsibility as soon as she went home.

I wondered how I was going to manage to run my house and look after this totally demanding and itchy child. It was necessary to prevent her from scratching too, because what new skin she had was fragile in the extreme and would rip and bleed with next to no provocation.

Well, I coped. It was not pretty, but I coped. Brian coped. Hiroshi had a bad reaction, which was to be expected, but he coped too. By July

I could handle Mura's dressings on my own so the kids and I packed up our Flamazine and stretch net and gauzes and flew out to spend a month with Mom. The annual thing. Mura whined and scratched and woke up in the night. Hiroshi acted out and sassed back and informed me that if I ever went to the hospital again, he was coming too. I lay around like a banana peel, kinda limp and empty and useless; too tired to biodegrade.

But still, if my Year From Hell had been a day, I'd have to say the month of July was the coffee break. Mom takes her coffee bone-corrodingly strong; one cup a day at five in the afternoon. We cordoned off the children—plugged them into the VCR—and indulged for thirty minutes. Mom had received a present from a friend: a box of good chocolates, little individually wrapped fingers with different flavors and fillings, lined up in twos. She doled them out, one a day, with our coffee. I'd sit there dipping the stick in my hot brew and sucking off the melted bit, until the sticky sliver finally dissolved on my tongue.

And then the kids and I went home, and, instead of dressing changes, Mura had rubs of pure vitamin E twice a day to minimize scarring. Shirley had sent her kids off to their grandparents' place for the summer, but traditionally, August was the month I did holiday relief work at the office. I badly needed to bolster my resources, so off I went. Working full time totally fractured what little semblance of structure we as a family had left, but that wasn't our biggest problem. The real kicker was Brian's job.

Heroic Raspberry Coffee Cake

Just as coffee always makes me think of my mother, raspberries will also be forever wedded to my memory of her. When we were growing up, Mom had a secret raspberry patch, and she would go there every afternoon to pick off another section. She was very possessive of her patch; not just any old body got invited in. We kids were allowed to come, but it was very buggy and thorny, and we had things of our own to do. I never could understand Mom's persistence. Yes, raspberries are delicious, but it seemed that she went to an awful lot of effort.

It's only now that I'm a mother, with children I love to fill with good food, that I understand her pleasure in filling up the jug hung around her waist. What a good mama, all alone in that quiet, green world, plucking juicy rubies one by one, precious to the tongue, gathering food for her family. A secret time, in between day's early buzz and day's work finally done.

Set oven to 350°F. Grease and flour a 13" x 9" pan.
Sift:
2 cups flour (white or brown, depending on whether you're feeding a purist like my sister, or a sinner like me)
1/4 teaspoon salt and
1 tablespoon baking powder
Beat:
1/3 cup soft butter
1 cup sugar
Mix in a separate bowl:
1 egg
1 cup milk (or water) and
1 teaspoon vanilla

Now, add wets and drys alternately to the sugar/butter mixtures, until the batter is combined. Pour evenly and quickly into the pan.

Spread
raspberries, fresh or frozen, over the top, enough to just cover the cake.
Bake for 30 to 35 minutes.
Cool five minutes.

Glaze with
1 1/2 cup icing sugar
4 tablespoons cream (yes, milk will do if necessary), and
1 teaspoon vanilla, mixed together.

Eat while warm, but never standing up. Sit down. It's better for the digestion.

TWENTY-SEVEN

Brian's job. Brian's job. Like death and taxes, that job had always been with us. I haven't said a whole lot about that job because this is my story, damn it! I aim for letting go of control, not taking it on. But the job was a real mixed blessing. The good bit was that the bills got paid. The bad bit—well, there was a list. Weird hours, unhealthy working conditions, loud music—those were to be expected. Part of the bar industry. But the petty little political games, the bounced pay cheques and the constant job insecurity—that we could have lived without. Why didn't We find another job? I don't know. It wasn't Our job.

I've said before that fear of unemployment is a lifestyle constant. This goes for me and all of mine. Recently, a group of my parenting buddies were hanging out at the beach with our babies. Out of seven families only one had a stable family income. Those are pretty poor odds. The economic sandstorm scours away at our social programs. No wonder. More and more of us are needing that safety net. It wasn't designed for this kind of traffic and volume. *Will I be one of those to fall through the cracks?* Yet we have a system based on widgets; consumption creates jobs. Planned obsolescence creates jobs. The excavators and caterpillars keep moiling downward, digging up Mother Earth for us to chew on, leaving us standing on a pile of slag. We eat the ground from beneath our feet and throw our waste over our shoulders like a wishing stone. The big machines keep rolling on.

I should pray for a revolution, but I'm afraid. (At bedtime Hiroshi brandishes a sword made of tinsel pipe cleaners. "I will fight the dark! I will fight fear!" "Make another one for me, please Hiro," I say.)

A few years ago, I started buying lottery tickets. I bought one every couple of months. I wouldn't check it right away. No. I'd carry it around with me, and on a nice day when I had enough spare change to waste on a new ticket, I'd take my old one in and check it. I'd buy again immediately. That way, I always had a chance in my pocket. At any time, I could be a winner. The possibility always existed that my financial worries were over, without my even knowing it. *My one-way ticket to La La Land.*

What made August so much worse? Maybe something to do with that screwing motion: Tighter. Tighter. Tighter. D'you like that? Good, 'cause here's some more! All August the rumors flew and in September, Brian's employers gave everyone a month's notice and put the club up for sale.

"Shirley," I said, "we have just reached a new level in terror. It's like peeling the skin off an onion until they've got us down to our begging bowl and our dhoti." I went out and got myself a Recession Haircut—clipped almost down to the roots. Lasts six months, needs half as much shampoo. Every time I heard someone use the words "welfare bum," I winced. Would they mean me soon? All my old garbage came in with the tide: waves of "should have, should have, should have." I should have got myself a profession. I should have made financial security a priority. Poor people shouldn't have babies.

Which is worse: being employed, or semi-employed, on the tread-mill, dead-end, round the circle, no way out—or being unemployed, looking, frantically looking, beating the street, no one wants you, in the maze, no way out? Answer: both. Either way, barely paying the bills, month by month. No room to give. No way out.

"It won't always be like that," chided friends in their forties whose children were teenagers. "Your kids will grow up and go to school, and you'll go to work. There's a light at the end of the tunnel." Is there? Really? Still? Or does the increase in the quantity of groceries you have to buy absorb any increase you might have in spare change because of working more and having fewer baby-sitters to pay?

Fear of poverty. Fear of the downward spiral. Fear of being unable to afford appropriate supervision for my children. Fear of having to give them latch keys. Fear that by the time they need a job, their most promising career move will be selling their organs to science. Fear that all our social programs will completely crumble, and that we'll be left homeless, sick and starving, panhandling on the pavement in front of the churches (massive stone heritage buildings, put up early in the history of our exploitation, gorgeous with flaming stained-glass windows), begging on the street in front of the churches in a godless society. Fear of poverty. Fear that what's happening in Africa, in Bosnia, in Mexico, in my own wretched back yard will happen to me. No work. No job. No life. Two kids.

It was an intense reaction, but short in duration. Fear is a horse I'm learning to ride. It's real, it's alive, it needs to be fed, groomed and watered. But I'll be damned if I'll let it take me to hell before I have to. I've got better places to go.

This all happened in the fall of a good apple year. Katherine dropped off boxes of organic fruit from her trees for me to sauce and I filled my freezer. I flipped through my folder of "recipes to try," checked over my stash of selections: apple bread, apple pancakes, apple stuffing. We became addicted to a cake made with thinly sliced apples mixed into a batter described as "loose"—no measurements were given. It cooked in half an hour and we could eat a whole pan in ten minutes. For every cake I made I had to slice an extra apple and coat it with sugar and spices for Mura and Hiro to spear elegantly with their forks, sitting stark naked at the table, like an emperor with his chubby wife.

One Sunday some friends took us for a drive in the country and we stopped by a plum tree growing in the ditch. The plums were lying on the ground, warm with the sun. "Go ahead, eat them," my friends said. "They've only been here since yesterday." My friends could guarantee that, as they'd cleared the ground of fruit themselves the day before and gone home to make jam. Having been European war children, they had no use for waste.

The kids and I stuffed plums into our bulging cheeks. They were sweeter and juicier, more succulent than any I'd ever tasted before. We gobbled fresh fruit; the juice ran down our chins and hands to our elbows. Mura lisped, "More plum please!" I broke them open with my fingers, the stones popped out like slivers. Such goodness. Such goodness.

I did not smoke.

★★★★★

By October, the club had found a new owner and we carried on in much the same way as before: weird hours, weird sleep patterns, job insecurity, political bickering, the occasional bounced cheque. Great. I made a list of emergency disaster planning. For example, if there was an earthquake, I had bottled water stashed in various places around the apartment. If there was a nuclear war, we would try to assemble at my mother's farm. If Brian lost his job and he couldn't find another one, the worst-case scenario was that we wouldn't be able to pay the mortgage and we'd lose our place. I would still be no worse off than most of the single mothers that I knew.

I covered every possible disaster I could think of; I wrote out pages and pages. Then I bundled it all up and filed it. I put an elastic band around my wrist. Every time I thought about fear and failure, I snapped the band. *"None of that!"* Every couple of days or so I'd haul out my file, sort and review, add and edit. And put it away again.

Enough is enough. We will cope. Or not. But we're doing the best we can. I can't guarantee my future, but today we eat. Bless this food.

★★★★★

Then I had my October crisis.

A reformed alcoholic once told me the following story about his descent into the abyss. He said that he went to hell in ten easy steps (more or less) and that on every step he called out in anguish to God, "How much more of this are You going to give me?" He said that a very frustrated God called back, "How much more of this do I have to give you?" Sometimes we are very thick.

I mention it because what happened in October was like a little holy post script. "Were you paying attention? Just to be perfectly clear, this is what I said."

I had given blood to the Red Cross. It was something I liked to do: you get to lie there on your back on those webbed, lawn-furniture-type cots and give a gift to humanity. Besides, I am as strong as a cart-pulling pig and they could probably ladle my blood out and it wouldn't bother me. Peasant stock. Anyway, in October I got a beautifully written letter saying, hey, not to worry, but I had failed a primary screening test.

There has been a lot of news coverage on the sins of the Red Cross, so I want to be explicit: the letter was tactful, diplomatic and clear. My subsequent blood samples had checked out fine, but I should see my doctor, and international policy stipulated that once a screening test had been failed for whatever reason, the party in question may no longer give blood.

It had been a difficult year. I'd been through a lot. I wasn't at my best. Plus I had PMS. So I hit the roof. I surrendered the use of my brain. I forgot that I had given blood to my insurance company only the month before, and that they certainly would never have given me insurance if I had something horrible like AIDS or hepatitis C. I forgot that I had two healthy children, which would have been almost impossible to achieve if I had carried HIV. I totally lost perspective. I cried and cried and cried.

When I finally finished my temper tantrum and rational thought returned, I went down to Chinatown and bought soba. I came right home and made myself a huge bowl of buckwheat noodles for longevity. Slivers of tofu. Rounds of green onion. Slices of mushrooms spread out in a fan.

"Yes," I toasted myself, "it's a weird little world. It's warped and perverted and living is killing me. But this is my home. I want to live. I choose life."

I went to see my doctor as soon as she could fit me in. She suggested the possibility of machine error. She explained that the primary screening tests were designed to pick up every little thing and they sort from there. She sent me for another blood test which checked out fine. The whole incident was a blip in my life. An emotional adventure of a few days.

I did not smoke.

★★★★★

In November, a couple of days before my one-year non-smoking anniversary, the newspaper ran a very disturbing article on Easter Island. Apparently, paleontologists have discovered that Easter Island was once a wealthy paradise with a vast diversity of plants and animals. The people who lived there began building the gigantic statues for which the island is now famous and (the scientists hypothesize) completely depleted the island's resources doing so. A barren, poverty-stricken scrap of land with a lot of big stone statues was the end result. The article concluded with a reminder of our own rising population and shrinking resources. The author wrote, "Easter Island is Earth writ small."

I was deeply affected. Oh, my children. What have we done? What have we done? I do not have a lot of hope.

Yet for their sake and mine, I must find a way to hold a positive world vision in my mind without being blind or stupid. Something to work toward—something to create. I am a woman who likes a plan. If we can see it, maybe we can make it. Keep the Earth alive, and survive ourselves.

I used to think it was my fault, these waves of despair and fear. I used to think that I had some sort of moral deficit. Now I realize that keeping the faith, the faith that the human species can survive, the faith that we're worth saving—that is real work. Our collective problems are so big, our personal ones so daunting, no wonder we're afraid! No wonder we succumb to apathy or hedonism or despair, no wonder we close our eyes.

Not to give up, simply to keep caring (cheerfully, gently, lovingly) is a skill to be practised, struggled for, prayed over. A fitting direction for all my tools and talents. And so, I choose those small means where I hope to make a difference. I do what I can. I let go of what I cannot do. And try not to grieve too much.

Maybe there is a God—a reason and a purpose—the universe, in spite of all our various forms of wickedness, unfolding as it should. Maybe there isn't and eventually we'll destroy ourselves, and the cosmos, infinite and calm, will quietly fold over the pimple that used to be Earth, and a great peace will prevail. Would that be so bad? Nothing but stars forever and ever?

But either way, I must keep trying. Keep working for a better world. It's the only thing to do.

On my nicotine-free anniversary, Susan, who had walked with me through the valley of my addiction many miles, took me out for lunch. We had chicken crepes in a delectable creamy dill sauce with salad and later, a chocolate mint flan. It was delicious!

I didn't smoke.

Chicken Crepes in Creamy Dill Sauce

That meal was so good, I felt inspired to try to make it for Brian. Time consuming, but, my, it was delectable.

First of all, make the crepe batter, because it's supposed to sit. Combine:
1 cup white flour
1/4 teaspoon salt
1 cup milk
2 beaten eggs

Now make the filling. Take a
skinless chicken breast and slice it into long strips. Also slice
onions and
mushrooms. Sauté the chicken and onions, and when they're almost cooked, add the mushrooms. When the mushrooms are tender, put the whole pan into a warm oven for safe keeping. Put the casserole dish you intend to use for the finished product in the oven too.

Also, you need a sauce. Start by making a standard white sauce. Melt a lump of
butter, and add
a couple of tablespoons of flour
Brown it up nicely on medium heat in a heavy saucepan. Add
milk
cream cheese and
dill weed
How much cream cheese? How much do you have in the fridge? If you don't have any, well, I guess you don't add any, but 1/4 cup or so is nice. When the cream cheese is melted, check for flavor. Add
salt
a couple of dashes of cayenne, and
pepper
Dry mustard always makes cheese taste sharper if you want to emphasize that flavor. When the sauce is about right, put it on the back of the stove on your lowest heat.

Now, I don't have a crepe maker, but if you do, I assume you know how to use it. Mine is an amateur production, remember. But then, if I can do it, so can you. So heat up your cast-iron frying pan on medium, grease it lightly with salad oil, and get a big platter to put your crepes on. When the pan is good and hot, use your ladle to pour in a crepe. Swirl the pan to make the batter thin. When the crepe looks cooked, take it out. Don't wait for bubbles, don't wait for it to turn brown. You don't want the crepes crisp remember; you've got to roll them up. Crepes cook fast, which is great because while they're cooking, the sauce is congealing, right?

So, quickly, whip off those crepes, fill them with chicken and some sauce, roll them up like little carpets, and place them in the warm casserole dish. If you have cute little canoe dishes, you can make individual portions, just like I had at that wonderful restaurant. But how many little canoes can you keep in your kitchen cupboards, I ask you?

Cover the casserole with the rest of the creamy sauce and pop it into the oven until you've got the table set and the wine out.

Whip off your apron, wipe the flour off your nose (or, if you want to look like you've gone to *a lot* of trouble, dab more flour across your cheekbones), and ring the dinner bell. *Bon appétit!*

TWENTY-EIGHT

Why are we so afraid of endings?

"Oh Hiroshi," I moaned one day, "I wish you could have known your Grandpa Howie."

"But I do know him, Mama! I know him in my heart."

I was at the park, entertaining myself by polling strangers one day and I met the grandfather of an incredibly beautiful boy who was playing pirate with great gusto. The child was so swashbuckling, so devil-may-care, with his halo of golden curls and his big black boots, that he made me think of the nursery rhyme:

> *Bobby Shaftoe's gone to sea,*
> *Silver buckles on his knee.*
> *He'll come back and marry me.*
> *Bonny Bobbie Shaftoe.*

The grandfather and I chatted away, admiring the little lady-killer with his kiss-me-blue eyes and his dashing, flashing sword, and after a bit, the old gentleman told me that his grandson had muscular dystrophy and probably wouldn't reach adulthood. And I asked him what I really wanted to know: "How do you cope?"

"Well," he said, "every day we have together is a beautiful gift."

The thought of my children dying is unbearable to me. I remember discussing mortality with one of my cousins when Hiroshi was a tiny boy. I told him being a parent was so much work that if Hiro were to die, I wasn't sure if it would have been worth it. All that emotional energy, all the pain, all the grinding effort, all the investment which would never reach fruition, and worst of all, the lasting, aching loss I'd carry with me to the end of my days.

"What is fruition?" asked my cousin. "Isn't today in and of itself enough?"

Of course, he was right. If today is not enough, what is? Our lives are just a string of todays. I feel I could not bear the pain of my children dying—but of course some day they *will* die—everyone does. They'll grow up, I hope—they'll be teenagers. Supposedly I will find a way to let go, let them grow. I hope I will; it's in my job description. God willing, Hiroshi will become a man, and Mura a woman. Eventually they will grow old. And inevitably they will die.

But supposing, like my father, their lives are cut short, as we say, in the flower of their youth? Is that so very, very bad? I myself do not wish to die at present but longer is not always better, or so they say. Perhaps it is possible that my father lived to the fullness of his season. Is life not rich with meaning and purpose, every day, regardless of the size, the shape, the dimensions of our little lives and the lives of our loved ones?

Yes, the population is exploding, and no one wants to hire us, but we each have a powerful light within us—I have seen it!—and there can never be too much of that inner light. Is it not a mission in itself to learn how best to let that light shine? And even if there is no God, no outside source or motivation to dedicate that light to, is that not all the more reason to light up the world? Every day. Minute by minute. In spite of evil. In spite of death.

Why are endings so hard for us?

Oh God, I miss you, Daddy!

But that's life, and life is hard. What do I want?! An easy life? A contradiction in terms! Not life? Death then! But no. I want my cosmic minute, my brief space upon this Earth. I want life, unpredictable, painful, scary as it is, and I want my children, even if having them means I could lose them at any time. "Every day we have together is a beautiful gift." God have mercy on us. Give us the eyes to see it that way.

And nerves of steel.

Toasted Sunflower Seeds

(Pre-food and After-dinner Nibbles)

This for the record: there are times when I like to think that the end is the beginning, and the beginning is the end. So here's a toast to pre-food and after-dinner nibbles of all sorts and kinds, the first thing you pop between your crunchers at a party, and the last flavor to linger on your tongue before you leave.

In a bowl combine:
2 cups sunflower seeds (or other seeds or nuts: **pecans, cashews, almond**s, take your pick)
1 teaspoon each garlic powder, salt, chili powder
1/8 teaspoon each cumin and dill
2 shakes cayenne
1 dash of oil (to make the spices stick)

Toast in the oven at 200°F, turning every five minutes or so. Good hot or cold.

TWENTY-NINE

This is my Treasure Box, which holds a joke, a recipe and a picture. Go ahead, look inside; I have put them there for you.

This is the joke that Brian and I made up together:

What did PeeWee Herman say to Jean Paul Sartre?

"I know I am but what am I?"

Part of what makes marriage so difficult is that men and women have totally different modes of communication. Like I always say, creating two sexes was God's way of making sure everyone gets a multi-cultural experience.

"Do you find living together incredibly difficult?" I asked Brian.

"That's an understatement!"

"Good," I said, "it's nice to know we're in the same boat."

"It's nice to know you've been trying too."

"Isn't it obvious?"

"Not necessarily! How could you know how hard I've worked to learn your secret language for you? How could I know what you've done out of love for me?"

These words are never said. Instead, I buy fresh bagels, and back bacon in neat, pink rounds. Whip yellow yolks and butter and lemon into a creamy sauce. Gently baste perfect eggs, sunny side up. The blue oriental pattern around the edges of the plates makes a reassuring border. With twists of orange, I serve this beautiful dish (but not too often; I don't want him to have a heart attack).

"Did you get my message?"

"I love you more than spaghetti," Brian said. It was one of the most satisfying moments of my life.

*****

Here is the recipe for my all-time favorite sandwich. Take a baguette or loaf and split it lengthwise. Grate sharp cheddar cheese or gouda. Mince onions. Chop black olives. Mix all the filling ingredients together with Dijon mustard. Spread with vigor over the baguette, and toast the whole thing in the oven. Make a thermos of strong, hot coffee and fill a bottle with lemonade. Wrap the sandwich in a clean dishcloth. Gather up your children (if you have them) into readiness and take them with your provisions to the beach. Don't forget the sand toys. Indulge, watching the waves and the babies. Smile.

*****

Here is a picture of me at this time in my life: Jo-as-Mother-of-Small-Children, standing on the sidewalk outside our apartment building with Mura (who is two) in my arms. Hiroshi is five. He stands beside me, wiping his nose on my sweater sleeve. I have the umbrella stroller hooked over my arm and in my backpack I have snacks, a change of clothes for both children, an emergency diaper, bus fare, safety pins, knife (for peeling apples), library card, pen and paper in case I have a brilliant idea for a poem or think of what we need to buy for supper. Behind us, our home: on the third floor and down the hall to the right, with its blankets and dishes and boxes of durable plastic toys, the clothes, the towels, the newspaper clippings, the bills, all my cooking paraphernalia, jars and jars of spices . . .

Outside, in the pale, late-afternoon light, the evening moon rises. The last autumn leaves, brown and rotting, festoon the rain-soaked mossy lawn. The rich, wet smell of summer's wealth decaying fills my nostrils.

All that I hold dear holds me down.

When I die, no doubt I shall be lighter than air. Like a puff of smoke, I will rise, oh so gently. Ethereal. Formless. Free. The tax man, he will not find me. The plumber I will never again need.

Such a short time to spend upon this Earth. Later, later, I will be lighter than air.

EPILOGUE — THREE YEARS LATER

Wanna know what happened? But it ain't over yet!

I am trying to write an epilogue and Mura has the puking flu. It's buckets, rags and ginger ale for me today. Same old marimba. Sometimes you party, sometimes you get stuck under the limbo bar.

Hiro is eight now, Mura is five. My toddlers are big kids—beautiful, independent, interesting big kids. I can talk on the phone without someone crawling up my leg or spilling something accidentally on purpose. I can't count on having time—someone will spike a fever or fall out of a tree for sure. But I can read, I can make supper, I can have coffee with a friend—I am in that golden period between infant-induced sleep deprivation and waiting up all night worrying about when my teenagers are going to get home.

People told me that the small-child stage wouldn't last long, even though it seems interminable when you're going through it. Not that I didn't love it, just that I thought I could get lost there. I didn't.

Yet in essence, nothing has changed. True, there are fewer shoes to tie, but my energies are still focussed on creating a healthy balance. Like that's easy or something. Constant vigilance springs to mind.

Shirley claims that kids don't stop needing their parents. They just need adult attention in different ways at different stages. She says that just before her teenage boys left home, they went through a phase where they drained as much energy off as infants do, except that it was a different kind of energy. I'm not sure what she's talking about, because I'm not there yet, but I guess I'm in for the long haul. We haven't seen the big bucks yet. Brian changed employers but he's still bartending; I'm still piddling around cleaning houses, sewing and doing odd jobs. It works. We survive. Our lack of a pension plan is a chronic nagging worry, but full-time employment, gee, at this point, I don't know. I get the job, I need after-school care for the kids, I need the car, I get the car, I sign my kids up for piano and soccer and tap, then I have to pay for that too, I'm driving around, I need quicker meals, I order out, I'm spending more money, I need the job . . . I've got no time and no more money than I had before, and I'm making a whole lot more garbage for posterity. Suit yourself, but I think I'd like to skip a few steps for as long as I can.

It still takes an amazing amount of time and energy to raise my kids the way I want to. For example, Mura can vacuum the floor under the table, and Hiro can rinse dishes after supper, but I have to direct them. It would be easier by far to do it myself at this stage, but I want them to learn to contribute to the maintenance of our family. I am told this will pay off in the future.

And The Ritual. We light a candle, name the parts of our day that we're most and least thankful for, and eat a snack together. Brush our teeth and read stories in bed. Again, it's a good ceremony, one that binds us together, but it doesn't just happen. I have to *make* it happen.

And I'm writing another book. I always wanted to write books. I tell myself I'm setting a good example. "Look, kids, you have a dream? Make it happen." Maybe someday I'll even make money! Wouldn't *that* be cool!

*****

I asked Brian to keep the kids out of my hair so that I could finish these last pages.

"What d'you need an epilogue for? It's a process. You want an epilogue, you've got to die."

And then he made "sick-soup," chicken noodle in a mug, for Mura and started a game of picture-wars with Hiro. They're taking turns drawing space battles on a big sheet of paper right now.

Our lives? Nothing happened, thank God. And have you noticed? The world hasn't ended yet.

I didn't smoke.